Cruise through History

ITINERARY 04

PORTS OF THE BLACK SEA

SHERRY HUTT

TABLE OF CONTENTS

PREFACE

Cruise through History is a collection of short stories grouped by the sequence of many popular cruise itineraries, rather than by country, or period of history. As the stories move from port to port, they randomly move through time. The stories are all true. They introduce the traveler to the history and culture of a port through the story of a long-ago, or not so long-ago, resident, whose exploits left a castle, a palace, or a lovely site that can be explored on a cruise ship shore excursion. In this volume, there is even a prison to visit.

The host character for each port stop is chosen for their inspiring actions, and the visible culture left behind. Some names will be familiar, presented in these volumes with depth to their personality. Other characters may become like new friends, too long unrecognized. They may inspire you to read further. Either way, the stories offer a new twist to the school-age history of a place, drawn together to put travels in a fascinating context for the short-term visitor.

No apology is made for the choice of subjects. They have been chosen arbitrarily on the whim of the author, accumulated from past travels, for your enjoyment. The desire is that the reader will share the fun. No attempt is made to be politically correct, or give a chamber of commerce gloss to the stories evident in the remnants of the past. Knowledge of history can teach us a great deal about ourselves and the human condition, but only if it is honest and fairly told.

No doubt, it is the quest for *real* that draws adults to travel as often and for as long as they are able. Travelers who found history in school to be dull, later in life seek to fill in the gaps in their knowledge, with personal experience. This is the opportunity for the events of one's life to give rich meaning to the human condition and to enjoy stories of fact for which fiction is no rival.

Praise is due to the many historians and other scholars who have delved deeply into source data to ponder the minute details of history for pedagogical pursuits. Such information has been mined here, with attribution in footnotes, for the lively details, which will heighten the traveler's enjoyment of the past. History is a public good. The more it is found to be enjoyable, the more it will be valued.

An apology is due to those who hoped to foster a disciplined scholarship in the author. This is reading for an out-of-the-classroom experience. Footnotes are inserted to give due credit to scholars who have provided valuable information and to remind the reader that these stories are true. The presence of source notes is not to feign an academic appearance. Editorial sidebars and fun bits are in the footnotes.

When there are gaps in the facts, or mysteries remain, they are not supplemented by fiction. Rather, an effort is made to look at the known as a guide to the unknown. The reader can draw their own conclusions, daydream through the gaps, and enjoy the reason that so much popular fiction and movies are drawn from historical facts.

These stories are offered to give historical context to the sites often visited as cruise destinations. In these stories, meet the characters who walked the same streets centuries in the past. Go beyond the castle ruins to envision the people who built them and lived there.

Itineraries in this series have stories at each port that seek to inspire cruise travelers to rise out of deck chairs and investigate a destination with honesty and irreverence, or the potential traveler to rise from the sofa and embark on a Cruise through History. There is no stigma of a school assignment. Earn an "E" for enjoyment.

Itineraries in the Cruise through History series available and forthcoming-

    I.   **London to Rome - Coasts of France, Iberia, and Northern Italy - 2014.**

    II.   **Rome to Venice – Adriatic, with Sicily, Sardinia, Corsica – 2014**

    III.   **Eastern Mediterranean– Greece, Turkey, Cyprus & Israel – 2019**

Find all the storybooks through cruisethroughhistory.com.

ACKNOWLEDGMENTS

Writing travel stories began as therapy from the world of Washington, D.C. Thanks are due to those at Utah State University, Logan, and the several cruise lines that have allowed me to share stories with guests and students. Much appreciated are those who helped to produce the series, including:

Digby and Rose, publisher, art director, and publicist; Heather Richmond, editor; and Lisa Lynn Aispuro's research assistance. Diana Verkamp, CTH logo.

These stories would not be possible without the treasure trove of material in libraries and used bookshops. In this increasingly paperless world, bookstores and libraries provide solace and an opportunity to revive our humanity.

Much appreciation is also due to those who apply their skill to preservation and protection of heritage resources in the United States and around the world. The greatest thanks go to my husband, Guy Rouse, who has lugged my camera equipment all over the world for thirty years.

This volume is dedicated to my travel buddies, all of you who have joined my travels and added to the experiences. So many good times, so many photos, have all become the fabric of memory and the inspiration for stories.

All photos in this volume are the work of CTH, accumulated over thirty years. Photos and art are property of Cruise through History©, and all rights are reserved, unless specifically indicated. No use may be made of photos, art, or text, the construction of history in stories, without prior permission of the author.

INTRODUCTION

LAYERS OF CULTURE AROUND LAYERED WATERS

The Black Sea area remains mysterious to many travelers from the United States. To visitors from England and Western Europe, the area is most often associated with mid-nineteenth century Crimea and Crimean War. In this land of Jason and the Argonauts, Medea, and Yalta Peace Conference at the end of World War II, ports of the Baltic Sea are often overshadowed in history by great world events and pervasive mythology. There exist intimate stories to intrigue visitors. Ports of the Black Sea require an introduction, before embarking on an itinerary.

American scholar of Black Sea economic and political history, Charles King, describes settlement of port towns of the Black Sea as layers of habitation by waves of cultures. When not waging war against each other, or importing plagues, the mix of cultures in relatively open societies greatly added to vitality and economic development of the area. From the millennium before Christ to the opening of the Suez Canal in 1869, Black Sea ports were at the center of world trade.

An unsettling dynamic over two and a half millennia of Black Sea history is, according to Professor King, the result of advanced port city economies existing within nationalistic, uni-cultured, and less economically vibrant countries. The vibrant ports of Odessa, Ukraine; Sebastopol, Russia; Sinop and Trabzon in Turkey; Batumi in Georgia; Sochi in Russia; Constanta in Romania and Nessebur and Varna in Bulgaria, all were impacted by actions occurring thousands of miles away in capital cities of empires that have waned, including the Ottoman Empire, Imperial Russia, and the Soviet Union. Often national rulers looked upon economic vibrancy of Black Sea ports as threatened independence asserted in far-flung reaches of their domain. Ironically, by stifling the port cities, in part by efforts to nationalize or homogenize the resident culture, those same rulers often compromised their income.[1]

---

[1]   Charles King, The Black Sea: A History, Oxford Press, Oxford, 2004.

The area around the Black Sea was home to several nomadic tribes before the historical, or mythical, Jason, assembled his sailors on the ship, the Argonaut, and rowed their way from Greece, through the Bosporus, to the eastern edges of the Black Sea, and then hastily retreated across the sea to the west seacoast and up the Danube. The Argonaut's goal was to find gold. Their voyage occurred in the mid-thirteenth century BCE, well before the Trojan War.[2]

From 800 BCE to 600 BCE, several Greek cities were founded on Black Sea coasts, as Greeks sought to stretch out from the crowded peninsula of home. In the Greek peninsula, society overpopulated their environment by 500 BCE. Greeks came to the Black Sea coasts to grow grain until almost the entire Black Sea coast was under Greek settlement. Eventually, trade expanded to include amber and furs from the Baltic, to spices from the Far East and Persia. Wealth of the Black Sea supported families in Athens.

Romans followed Greeks in the Black Sea, as they did across the Mediterranean landscape. Colonists from Megara in Greece settled in Chersonesos, outside of present-day Sebastopol, in the fifth century BCE. The city was enlarged by the Romans at the beginning of the Common Era. Chersonesos is the setting of a story at the port of Sevastopol as it was witness to over a millennium of development and is now an often-visited archaeological site. Trabzon, Turkey, settled by the Greeks in 500 BCE, became a Roman outpost, as did ancient Sinope, now known as Sinop. Both cities retain vestiges of Roman occupation, seen today, although their glory days ended with the expulsion of the Greeks in 1923.[3]

Across the Hellespont channel from Constantinople, leading into the Black Sea, was ancient Byzantium. In the seventh century BCE, Byzantium was a

---

[2] The notation BCE, before common era and CE, common era are used throughout, instead of BC and AD. The references are applied to events in Christian and non-Christian domains and areas beyond Christianized borders.

[3] In 90 BCE Pontic Greek Mithridates the Great, who conquered Iranian and western Black Sea tribes, after killing his mother and brother to take the throne, avenged his father's death by Romans, by killing those Romans he could not expel from Asia Minor. Greeks of Trebizon, now Trabzon, did their part to expel Romans. Turks who entered the area upon departure of the Romans expelled the Greeks in the twentieth century. Herbert J. Muller, The Loom of History, Harper& Brothers, New York, 1958, pp. 374-5.

Greek colony. By 330 CE, Romans made Constantinople a Christian Roman capital, from which they controlled the Byzantine Empire and proliferated the Eastern Orthodox Christian Church. With the spread of Christianity and the crusades of the eleventh through the fourteenth centuries CE, the area of the Black Sea came under Byzantine rulers. Until the fifteenth century, when Muslim Ottoman Turks overtook the Byzantine Empire, residents of Black Sea ports were predominately Eastern Orthodox Christians. Layers of history and domination left Nessebar with more churches per capita than most cities of the world.

The Black Sea became a world trading center in ancient times and grew in influence in medieval times, with trade dominated by Venetian and Genoese sailors. When the Venetian explorer/merchant Marco Polo returned from over twenty years of travels to strange and far off lands of China, India and the East Orient, he kept a journal. Upon his return through Trebizon, now Trabzon, and across the Black Sea to Constantinople in 1295, he ceased his journal. There was nothing new to report in the well-traveled area of the Euxine Sea. This peaceful commercial existence lasted until the Battle of Varna in 1444, when the Catholic world of the Black Sea fell to the Ottoman Empire and the domination of Muslim rulers from the East and the Far East.

Meanwhile, northern steppes of Asia were becoming more populated, as ancient people and new arrivals melded into what would become Russia. The Khazars were a people who traced their lineage to Noah. They moved west from the Caspian Sea, where they engaged in trade during the tenth century CE with tattooed Norsemen from the Baltic Sea, who are often called Vikings. The pale northerners were known as Rhosoi or Rus. They claimed Kiev as their capital.

As the story goes, the Khazars were ecumenical when it came to religion. Their leader called in a Christian, a Muslim, and a Jew and asked each to name the top two religions. The Catholics and Muslims each chose their own religion and were each ambivalent about the Jew, so by default Judaism became the Khazar's religion. Large Jewish populations flourished at northern Black Sea ports. Russia became populated by a blend of pale northerners and dark Khazars.

In the mid-eighteenth century, Catherine the Great of Russia unified her provinces and fought her way down to the Black Sea. As Christian Russia advanced, Muslim Turkey receded, until the north shores of the Black Sea were Christian, and a bit Jewish, and the south predominantly Muslim. Tensions at the boundaries on the east and west sides of the Black Sea resulted in occasional wars, where Christian/Russia met Muslim/Turkey. One of these wars was the Crimean War of 1854, in which Christian enemies, France and Britain, joined with Muslim Turkey to advance against Christian Russia and contain Russia north of the Danube. This is the setting for the story of the Bickering Brothers of the Crimean War, at the port of Sevastopol. If this introduction is confusing, it is because little of the war made political, or strategic sense. The world returned to the Crimean Peninsula in 1945, for the Yalta Peacce Conference at the close of World War II.

In the twentieth century, provincial nationalism took hold all around the Black Sea, as the Ottoman Empire dissolved by the end of World War I. In 1923, over 100,000 Christian, Greek-speaking, cultural Turks, whose families went back two and a half millennia in Trabzon, Turkey, were expelled to Greece. Greece reciprocated by sending to Turkey those Greek Muslims, whose people lived in Thrace for a millennium. In Russia, pogroms were making it difficult to be a Jew, forty years before Hitler invaded. Nazi extremism, of Germans and Romanians, reduced entire civic populations around the western Black Sea. In all cases, civic vitality was devastated in port cities of the Black Sea. Economic stagnation was exacerbated by Soviet Socialist control.

A further note is necessary to introduce the cruise passenger to the environment of the Black Sea. Before settlement by Greeks, the sea was known as *Axenos*, the inhospitable place. Greeks feared wintry storms that could cause waves to swamp boats and leave the traveler subject to hostile Scythian nomads on distant shores. After Ionian Greeks populated settlements around the sea, they dubbed it *Euxeinos*, a place friendly to strangers. This may have been more of a public relations campaign than reality. When the Ottoman Empire dominated its shores, the Black Sea was referred to as the *Turkish Lake*.

The Black Sea is fed by five freshwater rivers: Danube, Dnieper, Dniester, Don, and Kuban. Of those, the Danube flow is greater than the sum of the other four rivers. This causes a current to flow east from the Danube on the western side of the sea. The Black Sea is also fed by saltwater coming in from the south, with some velocity from the Aegean Sea, through the narrows of the Dardanelles. Jason and his Argonauts experienced unfavorable currents going west when they entered the sea, so they turned to the east. When they left Batumi hurriedly, pursued by Medea's brother, as the story goes, they fled toward the Danube and again fought a counter current.

Fresh and salt waters that feed the sea have not melded any better than competing cultures onshore. The heavier saltwater runs to the depths, and the freshwater comprises an upper sea layer. The lower ninety percent of Black Sea water is sterile. It is the largest lifeless water mass in the world. The upper ten percent has, until recently, contained abundant sea life, home to sturgeon the size of small whales. Until the advent of overfishing in the 1980s, a million tons of anchovies swam counterclockwise from Odessa and then back each year. Today the Black Sea faces environmental issues of water pollution and competition for diminishing sea life.

As in all Itineraries of the CRUISE THROUGH HISTORY© series, choice of stories is totally arbitrary. Ports of the Black Sea provide three millennia of options. Stories tend toward the lighter side of even dark phases of history, not to deny that evil has occurred, but rather, to highlight the endearing events that can provide enjoyable context to sights the traveler will visit.

CTH

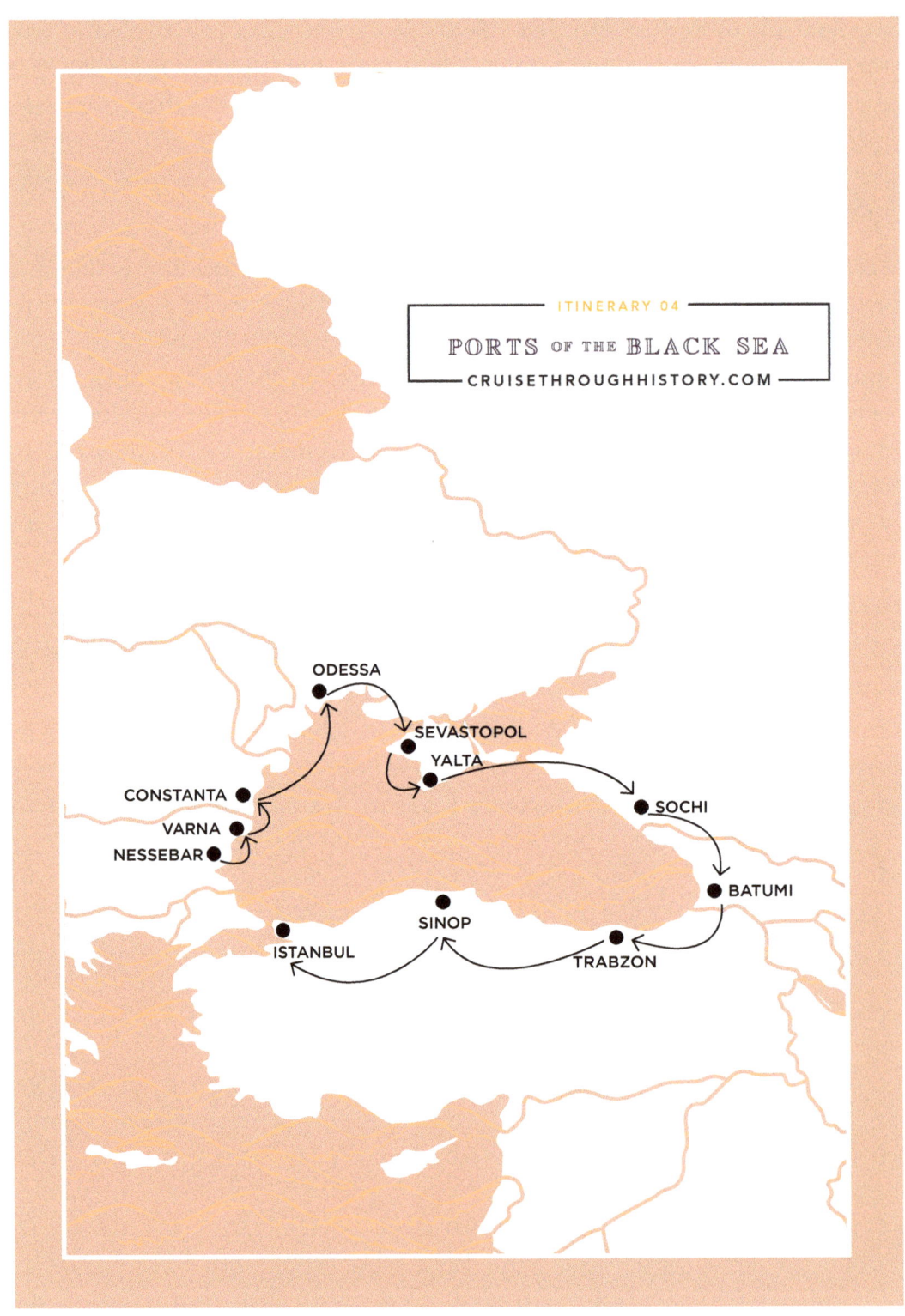

CRUISE THROUGH HISTORY
ITINERARY IV

Timeline | cruisethroughhistory.com

Ancient Era **Before 5th c BCE**	Greeks & Romans **5th BCE 5th CE**	Early Christian Era **6th c 18th c**	Recent History **19th c 20th c**
Jason &. Argo Chersonesos	Ovid Constanta	Nessebar Churches Varna 1444 Cyril & Methodius Odessa Trabzon Monastery Mosques of Istanbul	Sebastopol Light Brigade Yalta Vorontsov Palace Odessa-Pushkin Stalin's Sochi French Batumi Sinop Prison of Poets Modern Turkey

NESSEBAR, BULGARIA

(ANCIENT MESEMBRIA)

Nessebar: Most Churches Per Capita

Among cities of the Black Sea, with long Byzantine Eastern Orthodox traditions, Nessebar, Bulgaria stands out as having so many streets filled with churches for its small size, that per capita it has more than any other. Located on the western Black Sea coast, so close to the channel from the Aegean Sea, it is not surprising that this city was one of the first founded by Greeks in the sixth century BCE, or that so near the capital of Byzantium, it should be a leading center of Eastern Orthodoxy from the sixth century CE. Bulgaria today stretches inland to the north of Greece.

What comes as a surprise to the visitor, is the number, size, quality of preservation, and detailed ornamentation of such a large number of early Byzantine era churches in one small city area. The old city of Nessebar holds its story in stone streets and high stone walls. Forty Byzantine Orthodox churches survive there today.

Byzantine architecture, found all across the region from Russia through Greece and Turkey, is easily recognized by stone and brick buildings, where so often rows of clay-red brick alternate with light brick or stone. Arches alternate red and white brick. In Nessebar, small churches are Byzantine works of art, typically in dual-color patterns, inlaid with painted ceramics.

Church-building advanced over centuries from one long nave, with a bulging end for the altar, and a simple pitched roof, to more intricate churches with side aisles and side chapels, with high, many-pitched roofs and a tower. In Nessebar, streets are an open-air museum of evolving style. Even a street fountain and some homes are built in the dual color Byzantine style.

In the center of the old city stands a remnant of the fifth century, a large, many arched Basilica of St. Sofia, or as sometimes known, Hagia Sofia, the beautiful church. Even assuming the outer walls evident today were built over centuries, up to the ninth century, to create side aisles in the church and accommodate a growing congregation, this is still a massive church, given the time it was built and size of the city. Certainly, the Hagia Sofia of Constantinople is far larger and of greater grandeur. It had the emperor of Byzantium as a patron and sits in what was the largest city of its time. Nessebar was an outpost of Greek civilization, yet it too had a grand church.

Exploring the old city of Nessebar, with interpretive signs on every square, and in unexpected places on side streets, noting the date and significance of a church, begs the question of why here are there so many churches of such fine quality. When the United Nations designated Nessebar a World Heritage City, the award was made noting the examples of structures over time, which display a history of Byzantine Orthodox churches. The city is an open-air museum, telling its story.

A Little History of the Bulgarian Black Sea Coast

Nessebar has a population of less than fifteen thousand today, less than thirty thousand in the greater city area, despite having been continuously habituated for 2,600 years. It followed the historical path of its fellow cadre of Greek settlements from the sixth century BCE, established to feed Athens grain. The city, founded by people from Megara, now part of Athens, was known as Mesembria.

When Rome overtook Greece as master of the far empire, Romans came to Nessebar. Romans did not establish a great city with a large theatre as they often did elsewhere. They came late to Nessebar, probably in the first century BCE, when the Roman Empire was stretched thin from Britannia to Turkey. Often Romans enlarged Greek theatres with an elaborate stage. In Nessebar, the Greek into Roman ruin greets visitors from the docks. The site sits majestically overlooking the water, not as impressive as theaters in cities of the Aegean coasts, although impressive.

The high point of Nessebar came in the Christian era. The early Christian times of the sixth century to the medieval thirteenth century are amply represented in churches and houses. During the medieval period, a great wall was built around the city, with a fortress at the docks. In a city of great churches, the growth of trade spurred the need to protect residents within its wall.

Not surprisingly, Nessebar was an early city of trade. Sitting on the southwest corner of the Black Sea, easily accessible from the Danube to the north and land routes from Athens and Constantinople in the southeast and southwest, grain from Nessebar could travel by land or sea.

In the sixth century BCE, the usual means of trade was barter. In ancient times, where gold was plentiful, such as in northern Africa, certain goods like salt were weighed against gold. In Nessebar, gold was not an abundant commodity. Amber from the Baltic; spices, silk, and dried fruit from the east; and wine and olives from the south were exchanged for grain. A means to determine value in exchange was necessary, not dependent upon comparative weight.

Coins as the medium of trade began around the sixth century. Often Greeks are credited with the development of a standard value currency. Gold used as weights were often fashioned into standard-sized ingots. Those gold bits, flattened to heap on a scale, were made into stamped weights, in the name of a trading city or leader. They became coins of the realm. Historians of Nessebar give the city credit for the development and use of the first coins in the sixth century BCE. At that time, Nessebar was a Greek city and a major trade station. The attribution is credible. Coins have been found in Nessebar, stamped with the city emblem, dating to the fifth century BCE.

In the ancient Roman empire, Nessebar sat toward the northern edge of the Black Sea region, the extent of which was Varna. When the Roman empire split into regions, Nessebar was within the domain of Roman emperor Constantine, the first Christian emperor. When Constantine made Christianity the religion of the realm, Nessebar became an early center of Christianity. Possessing great wealth from trade, from the fifth to the eleventh century, Nessebar built Byzantine churches. Building in Nessebar coincided with the growth in power of the First Bulgarian Empire.

In the seventh century, tribes in Bulgaria coalesced into a powerful army. So effective was the military, under a succession of leaders, that the Bulgar forces kept at bay the Hungarian Magyars from the west and Arabs from the south. The territory of the First Bulgarian Empire extended from the Adriatic Sea, with a capital at Ohrid, south into Macedonia, to the full western banks of the Black Sea at the Dnieper River. Bulgars controlled traffic on the Danube River.

In the tenth century, the Bulgarian Empire was Christian, and its cities were bastions of Christianity and church-building. Ambition overcame Christian ethos, and in 923, the Bulgars lay siege on Constantinople. They crushed the Byzantine army, although not fatally. In the next century, Byzantines staged a come-back. The once-mighty Bulgarian Empire surrendered to Byzantine might in 1018, ending the First Bulgarian Empire. Byzantium was at its height.

Ivan the Great and the Second Bulgarian Empire (1331 -1371)

A Bulgarian Renaissance came in 1331, with the reign of Tsar Ivan Alexander. For forty years he ruled Bulgaria, in what has been dubbed the Second Bulgarian Empire. Not only did Ivan enable a time of peace and internal stability, but he also sponsored art and architecture. The fourteenth century was a time of construction of Byzantine churches throughout Bulgaria, notably in Nessebar.

Ivan began his reign by conquering territory lost to Byzantium. He arranged a peace treaty with Serbia, cemented by the marriage of his sister to the Serbian king. Serbia controlled what had been the western Bulgarian domain and its capital at Ohrid. Bulgaria held the land south of the Danube, and south along the Black Sea to the remaining area of European Byzantium, north and west of Constantinople. The total territory was less than the Bulgaria of the First Empire; however, it was stable, defensible, and still controlled lucrative trade from the Black Sea along the Danube.

Ivan Alexander fostered the arts in the creation of illustrated manuscripts in monasteries and painting. He was harsh on heretics, particularly several Christian sects, which existed during his reign, and fostered religious practice. As such, he is revered by the church and appears in church frescos of the middle ages. Church construction faltered during the later Ottoman era.

The economy of the empire surged during Ivan's reign, in part due to his treaties with trading domains. He strengthened relations with Venice, Genoa and Ragusa, known today as Dubrovnik. After a prior doge of Venice waged a destructive campaign on Constantinople in 1204, Ivan was wise to maintain good relations with the successor doge.

The downfall of the Second Bulgarian Empire was its continual battles with Byzantium over their common border. Fighting between the two leading Eastern Orthodox empires weakened both. As the Ottoman Empire came west, it was able to capitalize on weaknesses in Byzantium, nibbling away at its territory, until 1453, when Constantinople fell to Ottoman Turks.

After the death of Ivan Alexander in 1371, his son was unable to hold the empire together, despite decades of co-ruler status established by Ivan. Weakened by continual warfare, the Second Bulgarian Empire ended in 1371. When Byzantium fell, the Ottomans continued west. Bulgaria was part of the Ottoman Empire until liberated in 1878. Nessebar was united within Bulgaria in 1885.

Building Churches in Nessebar

Ivan Alexander was an avid fan of building churches and monasteries. He is due the accolade of builder king for a large number of churches that were built during his forty-year reign. In Nessebar, he endowed two monasteries: The Holy Mother of God Eleoussa and St. Nicholas, both of which stand as monuments to the era. Also built during that time in Nessebar were St. Theodore, St. Paraskeva, St. Michael/St. Gabriel and St. John Aliturgetos. Bright frescos in some of these churches exist today. The exterior of the churches, although not large buildings, are exquisite in detail, with ornamental brick and imbedded, painted, ceramic pieces, creating a mosaic in brick and clay.

The architecture of the Second Bulgarian Empire is so distinctive in its unique style that it has been called the Tarnovo Artistic School of architecture.[4] Tarnovo architecture is characterized by small churches, long and narrow, disproportionately high. They are dark places of penance.

The exterior of Tarnovo style churches is an explosion of artistic expression by builders in brick and stone. Tarnovo churches use arches in alternating red and white clay brick. The interior of churches had Greek-style columns, although more in use were internal arches of brick. Inside the churches are painted frescos. Outside the church, walls are studded with small ceramic cups and stars, to create designs solid in construction and fanciful in overall appearance. Tarnovo churches are like large shoe boxes, with ample false arches, ceramic trim designs, and few towers.

Exemplary of the Tarnovo Artistic School is the icon of Nessebar, the Church of Christ Pantocrator. The Church of Christ is larger than most churches in Nessebar, has a many-faceted roof of domes, a tower, and arches, and sits within a large garden. The church invites visitors.

Characteristic of the Tarnovo school in the Church of Christ is the use of brick design, at its most fanciful in Byzantine churches. The church is a riot of three levels of rows of arches, in descending height. Even the tower and vault above the altar are surrounded by small arches in alternating red and white. Although the Church of Christ is large by Tarnovo standards, it is long, narrow and high. Like all Tarnovo Orthodox churches, the entry door is on the west. There is a smaller door leading to the narthex, a small room at the back of the church.

The Church of Christ Pantocrator also has Moorish arches as exterior decoration around the rounded altar. The inclusion of Arab architectural elements is common in Bulgarian churches in the Second Empire. Even before the conquest of Bulgaria by the Ottoman Empire, Nessebar was an international city. Architectural styles were eclectic and Arab traders were frequent in town through its earliest history. Ceramic designs around arches

---

[4] Tarnovo in central Bulgaria is an ancient Greek city and an administrative center of Bulgar tsars.

and extended altars at the end of each church, rather than designs of a cross, are Arabic, or iconoclast touches, so different from Roman Catholic churches and even Eastern Orthodox churches elsewhere in the world.[5]

Visiting Nessebar Today

Nessebar began as a Greek outpost in the sixth century BCE. In 1900 CE, the city was still ninety percent Greek and Orthodox Christian, with a population of about two thousand. To preserve the old town Nessebar, a new city was developed across the isthmus in 1925. From the medieval fort walls, the new

---

[5] Iconoclasts during the seventh and ninth centuries, throughout Byzantium, are responsible for gouging the faces from Christian church frescos and mosaics in Greece and Turkey. When Ottoman Turks occupied churches and made them into mosques, they often covered human figures with plaster, rather than destroy the art.

Church of Christ Tarnovo Style

city and the resort of Slanchev Bryag, developed in 1958, is seen just beyond the Ferris wheel and beaches of the Bulgarian Riviera. A little train takes visitors across the isthmus today, from the old town to the new city.

Not only is Nessebar notable for the number of Byzantine churches in the old town, most amazing is the survival of Orthodox churches during the pendency of over four hundred years of Ottoman Muslim rule. The Ottoman Turks were known for religious toleration. That did not also equate to preservation or maintenance of churches, particularly the number of churches found in Nessebar today. To remain standing, the heros of today are the builders of yesterday.

In some cities, such as in Constantinople, which Ottomans renamed Istanbul, churches were repurposed to mosques. In those instances, minarets were added, such as around the Hagia Sofia in Istanbul. There were no minarets in Nessebar, unless they were quickly removed in 1878, upon liberation from Ottoman rule.

Nessebar remains a city with so many churches today owing to the solid initial construction of stone and brick. Houses today in Nessebar often replicate Byzantine church design in small, low, and dark dwellings, with rows of alternating color brick and stone. Houses have small windows and low roofs. Although some historic homes in old town Nessebar today maintain second floors of wood slats, stone and brick were and are the predominant building materials. Garden walls and streets are of stone. In winding streets of the old city, the absence of wood to feed fires contributed to longevity. Unfinished stone and brick exteriors do not require new paint or plaster for maintenance.

Nessebar was a market town. Today the little streets are lined with coffee bars and shops, as they have been for over two thousand years. Trade and affluence diminished during the Ottoman Era, despite its available routes for distant trade. In recent years, Nessebar is enjoying a resurgence of economic vibrancy, cultural expression, and visitation of people from across the world. Today, few of the churches have active congregations, while others are museum pieces that add unique historical flair to wanderings in the city. Today Byzantine churches are not so much places of penance as places for a pleasurable time in a walkable historic city of the Black Sea.

VARNA, BULGARIA

(ANCIENT ODESSOS)

Battle of Varna 1444 to 1453 in the Decade that Impacted the World

Two of the most important dates contributing to world history of consequence, emanating from the Black Sea, were 1444 and 1453. The Battle of Varna in 1444 was short-lived, decisive, and of lasting impact. In 1453, the previously victorious Ottoman army swarmed into Constantinople, ending the life of the Byzantine Empire, and sealing off Europe from goods from Asia to the Far East.[6] Christopher Columbus, born in 1451, was raised hearing sailors talk of finding a route west to reach the Far East, foreclosed from routes from the Eastern Mediterranean to luxury goods and spices in the Far East by the Ottoman Empire conquests of 1453.

The Battle of Varna is notable for exhausting the Vatican treasury, leaving the pope insufficient resources when the Principle of the Eastern Orthodox Church in Constantinople called out for help when Ottoman Turkish forces stood at the walls of the capital of Byzantium. Murad II, the Ottoman sultan leading the conquest of western Asia and into eastern Europe, is often touted as leading the battle of the Crescent of Islam against the Cross of Christian

---

[6] Byzantine Empire and Byzantium refers to the area surrounding the channel between Europe and Asia that leads from the Aegean Sea to the Black Sea. The city on the Black Sea of Byzantia existed when Roman Emperor Constantine took control of the region and established his capital at nearby Constantinople. Constantinople became the capital of the Byzantine Empire. The Byzantine Empire is somewhat synonymous with the Eastern Orthodox Empire of Constantine and successor rulers. Ottoman Turks nibbled away at the Byzantine Empire until by 1453 only the capital of Constantinople and a small area outside the city were remaining.

Europe. Murad may have laughed heartily at the thought. For him, conquest was his obligation as a leader of an empire that looked to conquest to expand its treasury. That the pope funded armies to halt Ottoman expansion brought the armies of the Cross to battle armies of the Crescent, in a race to dominate commerce flowing to Europe.

It is a fact that in conquered lands, Islam was the religion of the empire. Sultans built mosques and did not promote or preserve churches. However, Ottoman Sultans were ecumenical. Alternate religious practice was allowed, as long as all communities paid their taxes. Religious toleration did not always flow to later rulers, or in the establishment of modern Muslim nations. At the time when flags of orders of Christian knights marched across fields along the western coast of the Black Sea, the underlying motivation was commerce.

Varna on the Black Sea coast of Bulgaria was a Greek then Roman Settlement. The trade center in existence at the time of the great battle was demolished. For four hundred years, the area was quiet. Upon release from Ottoman control, in the nineteenth century, Varna experienced a reawakening. Its city, as seen today, is a nineteenth-century gem built as though budding from underneath a cloud. The prominent city building is the Eastern Orthodox Cathedral.

The Battle of Varna is often regarded as the last Vatican sponsored crusade. It was not the last military engagement to stem Ottoman advancement into Europe. Shortly after the Battle of Varna, Murad's successor stormed the fourth-century walls of Constantine and took the city of Constantinople. The Byzantine Empire had been in descent for some time. Once a military power, the Byzantine emperor lacked funds to buy the one new battle tool, which would have saved the city: the cannon. The Ottoman sultan used his purchase of this new tool to great advantage.

In the next century, Christian nations mounted a joint expedition, called to arms, although not funded by, the Vatican. In the Battle of Lepanto, in 1571, once again, flags of the Cross faced flags of the Crescent, this time at sea, off the Adriatic coast of Greece.[7] At stake was Italy and Hungary and access to the

---

[7] Catholic France, Spain, Genoa and Knights of St. John took part in the Battle of Lepanto. Miguel Cervantes was a young sailor during the battle, where he lost use of an arm. His adventures continue in Cruise through History© Itinerary I London to Rome – Port of Seville.

conquest of Europe. This time Ottoman advance halted at Greece. Thereafter, the map of the Ottoman world expanded only south through Egypt, until the twentieth century.

Until the twentieth century, the political map of the Black Sea, and surrounding lands, remained fairly constant as established between 1444 and 1453. These critical dates in world history are almost unknown to students in the west. Knowing a bit of this history explains why the port of Varna looks as it does today. This is that story.

Varna as Battle Venue

Roman Baths in Varna

Settlement of Varna was begun in the seventh century BCE, by pioneers from the pre-Greek trading power of Miletus, on the west coast of Turkey. Miletus was a great city in league with Troy and Ephesus. Varna remained a growing trade center long after Miletus was reduced to rubble in war. By the height of the Roman era, the last centuries BCE and first centuries CE, Varna was a larger city than its sponsor.

Known as Odessos by Greeks and Odessus by Romans, the ancient city of Varna benefited from the building glory of Rome, with large Roman baths and public structures. Most of Roman-era Varna has been lost in building the medieval and nineteenth-century city. The Roman baths are notable for size and preservation. They are a tourist venue today.

When Varna entered the Christian era, the population warranted several basilicas. St. Andrew was reported to preach in Varna in 56 CE. By the time of the Ottoman invasions, there were ten Eastern Orthodox Basilicas and numerous smaller churches throughout the city. The name of the city changed with the times to Varna; the highly successful city on the Varna River.

During the millennium of the Christian era in the fourth century to the fall of Byzantium in 1453, tsars of Bulgaria and emperors of Byzantium, two large Christian domains of the Black Sea southern and western coast, were often at war over land. Interior land along the rivers Danube and Varna were grain-growing regions. Grain fed growing city populations and the coffers of their rulers. War depleted populations and emptied treasuries, facts that did not impress tsars and emperors in the Eastern Orthodox world until the Ottoman Turks arrived.

Varna sat on the line of two cultural worlds: that of Eastern Orthodoxy and the Latin, Roman Catholic Church. In the eleventh century, the Great Schism divided people between the two Christian cosmologies, occaisioned more by political control than religious dogma. This was also the time St. Cyril and St. Methodius came through Varna, preaching that with the advent of local language, people could read scripture without the aid of a priest. Priests felt threatened.

Cyril developed written Slavic vocabulary, which made him a heretic in Byzantium and welcomed in Rome. Before written Slavic language, only priests knew scripture. They held great power over the people. With language, Slavic people engaged in contracts, furthering trade, and commercial development.

In the late fourteenth and early fifteenth century, Varna was one of the largest cities on the Black Sea, behind Constantinople. Its forces were battle-hardened by skirmishes with Byzantium. Varna resisted late fourteenth century attempted conquests by Ottoman Turks, coming up from the south in modern-day Turkey, and Tartars, coming down from modern-day Ukraine. Its ports were active and its large citizenry prosperous. Varna was a prize to be taken by empires of conquest.

Battle of Varna 1444

Ottoman Sultan Murad II was forty when he led massive forces to take Varna in 1444. Born in 1404, he had been sultan since he was eighteen. His reign was studded with battle victories and enlargement of the Ottoman Empire. At age twenty-nine, he married Mara Brankovic, the Christian daughter of a Serbian king. The marriage did not spare the bride's father exemption from the Ottoman conquest. Mara remained Orthodox Christian during the life of Murad and supported churches throughout her life, even when, as a widow, she turned down a marriage proposal from the emperor of Byzantium and remained loyal to her step-son, Mehmed II.[8]

In 1442, Murad II entered into a ten-year agreement for peace with Hungary. Then he retired and turned the empire over to his twelve-year-old son, Mehmed II. Pope Eugene IV seized on the opportunity presented by the absence of the old warrior and reneged on the treaty.

Led by the young king of Hungary, the pope rallied kings of Poland, Moldavia, Lithuania, Bulgaria, Croatia, and the Teutonic Knights to join in pushing back borders of the Ottoman Empire. When Murad learned of the pope's plans, he came out of retirement to lead Ottoman forces. As a sultan, the son ordered his father into battle.

---

[8] Mara Brankovic was born in 1416 and died in 1487. She was known as an advisor to Mehmed II, and credited with negotiating peace and trade agreements with Venice on behalf of the Ottoman Empire.

Forces of the Vatican were twenty thousand strong, to face sixty thousand elite Ottoman Janissaries and mercenaries of the well-funded sultan. The pope planned that papal, Venetian, and Genoan naval forces would blockade the Dardanelles, the maritime supply route for Ottoman forces, while the Hungarian king would lead the troops in a land battle. Despite the greater Ottoman forces, forces of the united kingdoms fought well and landed early victories.

In aide of the united forces crossing the Danube, the real-life Vlad Dracula was the hero of the day. Dracula, the king of Wallachia, modern-day Romania, contributed four thousand troops, plus expert guides, knowledgeable of the terrain. They were joined by Poles and Russians from western Ukraine. As they marched through lightly-guarded, Ottoman-held towns, Ottoman slaves were released, to join the army. Some towns were taken with no resistance. When Murad learned of Dracula's success, he dug deep into his treasury to hire mercenaries as a sacrificial, overwhelming force.

On November 10, 1444, the two armies faced off outside of Varna. Valiantly, the Hungarian king led his troops, piercing Janissary lines, in an attempt to reach Murad. At the height of battle, the king and sultan were face to face. They crossed swords. Then, surrounded by Janissaries, the young Hungarian king was killed.

Records of the otherwise well-documented battle are vague on whether the body of the king was recovered. Some local stories hold that the king was quickly buried in a churchyard. Other legends tell of a king, left to live by the Ottomans, went into hiding, so demoralized by the loss in the battle that he hid from the world until his death.[9]

Hungarian troops, demoralized by the loss of their heroic king, fell into disarray. In the pandemonium of battle, the day turned into a slaughter. The battle was a decisive Ottoman victory.

---

[9] More likely neither legend is true. It is highly unlikely the Ottomans would restrain themselves from execution of the king. Inability to recover a body for Christian burial was fodder for any number of rumors.

Vlad Dracula King of Wallachia

Ottoman forces took Varna and increased their landholdings. The allied forces lost half their number, about ten thousand troops. Casualties among Ottoman forces were twice as many in number, representing only one-third their army. Facing forty thousand of Ottoman troops, the ten thousand forces under the papal banner disbanded and headed home.

Some estimates of casualties in the united papal forces run much higher. Several thousand troops were taken prisoner and either died of wounds, in slavery, or under torture. One fact is undisputed: Varna and most of Bulgaria was under the Ottoman rule for the next four hundred years.

The Fall of Constantinople 1453

After the Battle of Varna, Murad II attempted retirement a second time. His son, Mehmed II, also known as Mehmet or Mohamed II, proved not quite up to the task of leading an army, so dad resumed control of the forces. Only Murad's death in 1451, kept him from riding victoriously into Constantinople. That honor was left to his son in 1453.

Ottomans cut away at the Byzantine Empire for decades. By 1453, the only territory of the once great Byzantine Empire was the immediate area of Constantinople, southern Greece, and some non-contiguous land west of the city on the Black Sea coast.[10] The Renaissance in Italy inspired Byzantine intellectuals, artists, educators, and entrepreneurs to leave home for more vibrant venues. By 1453, only about five thousand men within fighting age remained in the city.[11]

In 1452, Byzantine Emperor Constantine XI made a decision, that he would live just long enough to regret. An iron foundry engineer from Transylvania, Orban Urban, designed a really big gun capable of knocking down city walls of stone.[12] He knew he had a marketable item and was looking for a client who could produce the guns. He offered the gun, now known as a cannon, to Constantine XI. The last Byzantine Emperor had no funds left in the treasury with which to purchase and produce Urban's guns.

---

[10]   Colin Wells, Sailing from Byzantium, Delta, 2006, including wonderful maps.
[11]   Jason Goodwin, Lords of the Horizons, Henry Holt, 1998, p. 29.
[12]   Urban lived in the Hungarian Empire, in an area now part of Romania.

Urban took his drawings of the cannon to Mehmed II. The Ottoman sultan was intrigued. He had an immediate need for the guns, and he could pay Urban's purchase price. Most important, Mehmed had the capacity to go into full production of the guns to arm his Janissaries.

Mehmed set up an iron foundry in 1452, near Adrianople, on the far western border of what had been the Byzantine Empire, which was by that time part of the Ottoman Empire. With Urban in charge, within three months, the Ottomans had a supply of cannons. They pulled the big guns on ox-sleds within range of Constantinople. Cannons became the new technology of warfare,

without which Mehmed II's ability to conquer the capital of the Byzantines would have been frustrated.[13]

In March 1453, Mehmet II began his siege of Constantinople. He called for the city to surrender. To back up his request, three hundred thousand fighting men accompanied Mehmed. Constantine XI felt duty-bound to hold tight the last Christian city in the East.

Constantine XI was not without resources to protect Constantinople, despite a lack of soldiers in the city. All of non-Ottoman Europe sent soldiers to assist, including Venice and Genoa.[14] A chain was placed across the harbor that was effective to keep out enemy ships. The city walls of Constantine the Great still held firm, improved by Emperor Theodosius, a millennium before. The walls had never been breached since built under direction of Emperor Constantine in the fourth century.

From the beginning of March to the end of May, Mehmed attacked Constantinople. He was not able to breach the walls, enter the harbor, or succeed in obtaining a negotiated surrender. Big guns fired at walls during the day, which were repaired from within at night. Janissaries swarming the walls were rebuffed. Mehmed was in danger of losing prestige among his people. Byzantium was thought to be a weak opponent. The city should have fallen quickly.

Out of desperation, Mehmed maneuvered his victory. First, he had his Janissaries lug longboats up the eastern side of the Bosporus, until they reached the coast above the chains in the harbor. Then the boats were launched into the water, filled with Janissaries, and rowed to the shores of Constantinople. On the western, inland side of the city, at the weakest point in the system of walls, Mehmed had his army drag several cannons into position.

Once more, Mehmed asked the city to surrender. When it did not, shelling by cannon filled the air with smoke.[15] A small breach was opened in the wall, allowing fifty thousand Turkish soldiers to enter the city. Constantine XI was last seen stripping off his royal insignia. He jumped into the fight to stem the breach.

---

[13]   Urban was at the scene of the siege of Constantinople, training Janissaries in the use of his cannons, until one blew up in 1453, taking his life.

[14]   Kaffa, on the Black Sea, was a Genoese colony. Battle was about trade and profit, not religion.

[15]   Cannons could be fired seven times a day. One cannon ball could sink a ship.

Citizens of Constantinople ran to the Hagia Sophia for safety. Janissaries killed everyone in reach as they followed screaming crowds of mostly women and children into the Hagia Sophia. Inside the church, the death toll was staggering. Bodies were piled high. The Byzantine Empire died that day with Constantine XI at the helm.

Visiting Varna Today

Varna continued as a trade port into the Ottoman era. Ottoman sultans were wise to leave local control to city managers, as long as taxes were timely paid. Cities that swore allegiance to the sultan were spared devastation and slaughter of the population. During the sixteenth and seventeenth century, the population of Varna grew. A fair characterization of the period would be that the city did not thrive. Foreign lords made no substantial investments in Varna, as one of many outposts of the empire.

In the eighteenth and early nineteenth century, Russia came south, seeking to break Ottoman control and seize the city. Varna was held for a while by Russia, then released to the Ottomans. Churches were built during this interlude of Eastern Orthodoxy in the Russian overlord.

Early in the nineteenth century, Varna was still a Greek city. When Greeks in Greece mustered to fight a war for independence from Ottoman hold in 1821, Varna was a center of Greek patriotic fervor. Greek freedom fighter, Alexander Ypsilantis, born of a noble family with estates along the Danube, and an officer in the Russian Calvary, came to Varna, where he stirred quite a bit of excitement for the Greek cause. Ottoman officials quickly rounded up his followers and executed them. Fifty years later, after the liberation of Bulgaria, most ethnic Greeks left Bulgaria and were replaced by Bulgarians from the interior. Today Varna is over ninety percent ethnic Bulgarian.

When British and French troops came to the Black Sea to fight the Crimean War in 1853, they chose Varna as a staging area. Before they arrived in battle, European troops suffered a plague with locals. After the war, a railroad was built connecting Varna down the coast to Istanbul. The new era of travel was rail. Varna grew in manufacturing, as well as trade. The seaport remained active.

In 1878, Ottoman rule dissolved and Varna joined an independent Bulgaria as a major city of under thirty thousand population. Bulgaria went on to suffer as a result of both World Wars. At the end of World War I, territory of Bulgaria was lost to Romania. At the end of World War II, the Red Army advanced on Bulgaria, and it became part of the Soviet Union.

In the dissolution of the Soviet Union, independent Bulgaria retained its industrial economy. Varna is an industrial city, with close trade relations with Russia. It is also a tourism venue, enjoyed by interior residents coming to the sea and cruise visitors arriving at its new port.

Pre–World War Varna

The city that greets cruise visitors is largely a center city of gracious nineteenth-century buildings, built during the brief period between independence from the Ottoman Empire and the First World War. Beyond the old city is a modern city of industry and a dense population. Vestiges of ancient Rome are seen in the baths. The Christian era is represented by Orthodox churches.

Architecture in Varna is an interesting mix of Ottoman and European, dotted with Italianate villas and Russian style Orthodox churches. Varna has signature buildings, such as the Archaeological Museum, featuring a gold hoard from the ancient Greek era, in an Italianate mansion, and old city streets of clubs and coffee bars in Art Nouveau buildings of French influence. The train station is of Russian Art Deco, strident and imposing, with clean lines. Varna is an international city, the composite of which is uniquely Bulgarian.

Bulgarian culture is a fascinating mix of Slavic and Russian. Bulgarians enjoy their thermal seawater baths and gardens. New apartment buildings attest to an economic upswing since 1990, and the growth of higher education, particularly centers for research of the Black Sea, make present-day Varna a vibrant port city. Bram Stoker's *Count Dracula* would no longer find Varna a dark, dank mooring spot for his ship *Demeter*. Sophisticated, yet low key, Varna presents a unique experience for wandering cruise visitors.

Varna's Russian Art Deco Train Station

Cyril and Methodius Empower Slavic Culture with Language

If ever there is a doubt of the power of the written word to unify people, civilize their social structure and deliver them from slavery, consider the plight of southern Slavic people before the ninth century of the current era. Disparate bands of Slavs, roaming western reaches of the Black Sea, were marginally communicating in a cryptic sense between bands, leaving them vulnerable to enslavement by stronger, organized civilizations, which included the Byzantine Empire. Around the periphery of the Slavic world, other peoples were developing cities and market centers. Slav bands remained as barbarians, enslaved by literate cultures.

Slavs, in the larger sense, are the predominant group of Eastern Europe. From the seventh to the eleventh century, Old Bulgaria, a land of Slavs, stretched from the Black Sea to the Adriatic, encompassing much of present-day Bulgaria, Macedonia, Montenegro, Serbia and southern Russia and Ukraine. The Byzantine Empire, including Greece, was at the southern border and Croatia and Hungarian lands were to the north and west. The Great Moravian Kingdom of King Rastislav, who ruled from 846 to 870, was actually a small area at the center of Old Bulgaria, known today as the Czech Republic.[16] Old Bulgaria of this story included Varna, Nessebar, Constanta, the site of Odessa and a slice of Crimea, including Yalta, which at the time of this story included Chersonesos.

---

[16] See www.americancatholic.org, accessed June 18, 2012 and Dec. 11, 2019. Also, the Catholic Encyclopedia.

Into the literal darkness of Slavic people, two brothers came, sent by the Emperor of Constantinople, to convert Slavs and baptize them in Christianity. Easily done, if only facial conversion from pagan to Christian; the brothers quickly realized that, wherein past missions learning language of Khazars or Tartars facilitated conversion to Christianity, for the Slavs, who lacked written language, and held only cryptic spoken language of an infinitesimally small vocabulary, lessons in scripture was a tool to develop the means to communicate, operate in a market economy and, in short, civilize bands into a unified people. For Slavs, Christianity could be a tool, not an end goal. The concept of enlightenment entered a non-religious sphere.

Basilica of San Clemente Rome – Place of Tombs of Saints Cyril & Methodius

Before the brothers Cyril and Methodius could translate scripture into Slavic language, they needed to create written language, then build a vocabulary in sounds audibly palatable to their new students. Slavs lived between the Latin and Greek world, yet did not understand either language. Written communication was beyond their experience. Cyril looked to the Lord for guidance. It came to him that, *in the beginning, there was the word*. He went into a monastery to create words, letters, and language for Slavs. For this effort, the brothers were canonized.

Once Cyril created a script of forty-one letters, many derived from Greek, he combined them into words to create a vocabulary of concepts known to Slavs. Gradually, vocabulary was expanded to include Christian concepts. Eventually, the brothers translated scripture into Slavic language. The new language was known as Glagolitic, meaning to speak and write. It was a precursor to Cyrillic script known today and Slavic language. Cyril earned sainthood as the man who gave Slavs literacy and the Bible. Language united Bulgaria and made it a cultural center for Slavs.

Not everyone in the land appreciated Cyril and Methodius. Pagan Bulgarians attacked Christians. German priests held great power over illiterate people, who could only view their mystical ceremony, performed in Greek or Latin. Stalwart priests felt so strongly that the word of god could only be heard or written in Latin, Greek, or Hebrew, that the brothers were ambushed on their travels. Only protection by Pope Nicholas I spared the brothers, as they continued to travel between Rome and Constantinople, through lands of Old Bulgaria.

This is the short story of the power of language to unify a people, civilize an identifiable nation, and enable resilience from slavery. It is the story of two brothers whose legacy is language and literacy, which gave identity to Slavic culture. The lessons of Saints Cyril and Methodius transcend religious ideology. Selfless and courageous, they are deserving of a little story.

Travels of Two Brothers from Thessalonica to Constantinople

Constantine, who took the name Cyril as a monk late in life, was born in 826, and his brother Methodius, baptized as Michael, was born in 815 in Thessalonica, an ancient coastal city of Greece, north of Athens.[17] Their family

---

[17] Also known as Salonica of Macedonia, the city has a long history as a Jewish settlement. Macedonians do not consider themselves Greek. As non-Greeks, Macedonians were part of the Byzantine Empire, which looked for religious direction to the Principle in Constantinople rather than the pope in Rome.

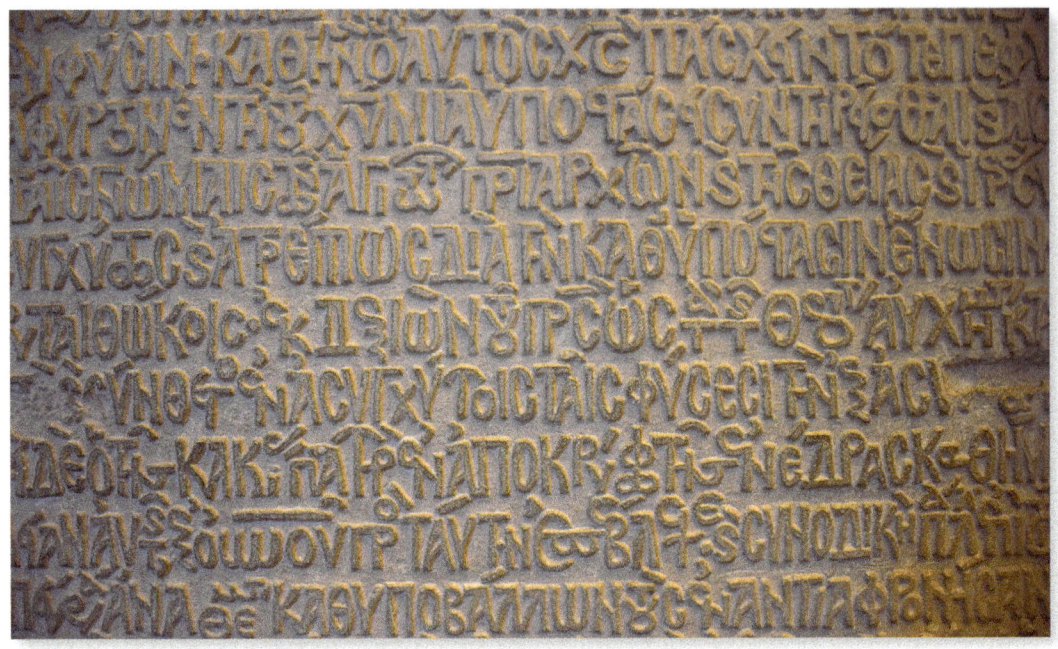

Early Writing Preserved in the Hagia Sofia Museum

was of political status. Little is known of their mother, although she was thought to be Slavic. The boys and their five male siblings lost their father when Cyril, the youngest, was fourteen. The family was fortunate to have a powerful protector, a government official, who fostered their education. Methodius, a talented artist, served as a government administrator, likely out of responsibility to the family and in gratitude to his surrogate father.

Cyril turned to religious education. He learned Arabic and Hebrew. In early travels on church assignment, he went to Chersonesos, lived in Arab communities, and sought to develop an open relationship between the Caliphate of Islam and the Christian community. Unable to convert Jewish Khazars, whose king allowed Christians, Jews, and Muslims to live peacefully together in his kingdom, Cyril wrote angry diatribes to his bishop disdainful of the spread of Judaism around the Sea of Azov.[18] He also learned the Khazars language to better attempt their conversion.

---

[18]   Khazars are a group from west-central Asia that came into the region of the North Black Sea as nomads in the sixth century and settled.

Inner Courtyard of San Clemente Rome

By 860, Cyril was in Constantinople, where his brother was abbot of a Byzantine monastery and an official in Byzantine governmental affairs. King Rastislav of Greater Moravia, requested the Byzantine Emperor in Constantinople to send teachers of Christianity to his people. The request was less a call for Christianity than a means to unify his people. In 862, the emperor sent Cyril and Methodius. Rastislav had no idea of the brilliance of his request.

In this instance, the people were not pagan. They had learned of Christianity from German priests, who held power over the people from the pulpit. Rastislav wished to be independent of German influence. The emperor in Constantinople appreciated the opportunity to send missionaries from his domain, rather than have the area between Constantinople and Rome be ministered to by the pope from Rome. Two centuries before the Great Schism, which split Eastern Orthodoxy in Constantinople from Roman Catholic under the pope in Rome in 1054, the two cities were in competition for dominance over souls.

The brothers traveled through the country of what is today Bulgaria, Romania, Bosnia, Macedonia Serbia, and Slovenia, and realized the people had no knowledge of Latin or Greek, nor did they have a local language, written or spoken, though they were all Slavic people. By 867, the brothers undertook to work with monks to devise an alphabet and form words to represent concepts.

When German priests learned that not only had they been usurped as religious leaders, but that the teachers were creating literacy among the Slavs, and worse, writing psalms in the new language, they accused the brothers of heresy for allowing scripture to be written in other than Greek or Latin. The Germans spiced their complaint by further allegations that the brothers had altered scripture. Dodging groups of armed men sent by the priests to murder them, and murderous bands of pagans, the brothers traveled to Rome to meet with Pope Nicholas I.

In Rome, the pope welcomed the brothers. Nicholas I was not opposed to the mass spoke in other than Latin and welcomed the possibility of the spread of the faith. He was also pleased to receive relics of St. Clement, brought by the boys to Rome, which enabled founding the Church of St. Clement.[19] Today that small church in Rome is the St. Clement Basilica, which has a chapel to Saints Cyril and Methodius and holds their burials deep within subterranean vaults. The timing was ideal for the brothers. Pope Nicolas I died in 867. Later popes agreed with the Germans that mass could only be spoken in Greek or Latin.

---

[19] Pope (Saint) Clement I died in 99, while in Chersonesos, where Cyril traveled on his first mission. Cyril believed the remains were those of the saint, who was martyred by drowning tied to an anchor. The remains were found preserved with an anchor.

By early 869, Cyril died. Never robust, he was exhausted by travel and efforts to create a language for the Slavs. Methodius returned to Old Bulgaria, as a missionary of Pope Adrian II, who elevated him to an archbishop. Shortly after arrival, Methodius was apprehended by German clergy and held captive for three years.

Methodius was freed by the intervention of Pope John VIII, who supported efforts to educate the Slavs. The papacy of John VIII was filled with defending Christians in eastern Europe from the advance of Muslim control and dissension in Constantinople, where the emperor wished to appoint the head of his own eastern church without intervention from Rome. Pope John VIII conceded to Constantinople's wishes and recognized the head of the eastern branch of the church, to be the Principle in the east, appointed by the Byzantine emperor.

In 879, Pope John VIII affirmed Methodius as archbishop. The seat of the archbishop was Nitra in Slovakia, where Methodius employed the script that he and Cyril developed. Methodius was in constant disagreement with German and French clerics over his insistence on saying mass in Slavic language. Upon the death of Pope John VIII in 882, the appointment of Methodius was in constant jeopardy. After the death of Methodius in 885, his successor was unable to obtain the support of Pope Stephen V. Within the year, the mass reverted to Latin all through Old Bulgaria.

Glagolitic Becomes Cyrillic

Cyril's first alphabet was a combination of the few existing symbols recognized by the Slavs and Greek, Hebrew and Samaritan, the later an alphabet Cyril became familiar with while in Chersonesos. The new alphabet and vocabulary became known as Old Church Slavic.[20] Read from left to right, phrases created by words of the new alphabet utilized a Latin rather than Arabic or Hebrew form. To identify numbers, rather than utilize Roman numerals, Cyril listed his alphabet in order, and numbers corresponded to the order of the letter.

---

[20] A shrinking minority of theologians regard St. Jerome as the originator of Slavic language.

Cyril was sensitive to sounds made and understood by Slavs. As he expanded their vocabulary, Cyril created words expressive of thoughts or concepts, rather than a list of names for objects. He wanted words to sound familiar to the ear of his students. By using a word for a concept, learning scripture was facilitated. To accusatory German and French clerics, the new vocabulary was construed as heretical alteration of scripture.

Old Church Slavic grew in vocabulary and usage for twenty-three years, from 863 to 886, before it was banned by the new pope and shunned by clerics. When Slavic language left the church, it flourished in the secular arena. King Boris of the Slavs saw language as not only a means to unite his people, disdain for Slavic by clerics enabled him to separate his kingdom from dominance by clerics and from Greek Constantinople. Language was liberating and unifying for Slavic people.

In the decade before he died in 889, King Boris of Bulgaria founded academies of learning in Ohrid and Preslav. The old Roman settlements flourished as though reborn. In Preslav, Bulgaria, students at the Preslav Literary School continued to refine Old Glagolitic into what is recognized today as Cyrillic. Glagolitic persevered in Croatia until the nineteenth century, when it was subsumed by Cyrillic, leaving the old language in church services. Cyrillic writing spread through eastern Europe and Russia, with Christianity and in spite of the Christian church in Rome or Constantinople.

Legacy of Saints Cyril and Methodius

Cyril and Methodius were canonized by fiat of their followers shortly after death. Cyril was regarded as a saint during his funeral procession. Pope Leo XIII was the first to record Saints Cyril and Methodius in church documents in 1880. Regarded as Patrons of Europe and Apostles of the Slavs, there is no doubt that the brothers introduced Slavs to literacy and gave them the gospels in a language they understood.

The path of Cyril and Methodius across the region of Old Bulgaria can be traced today by the presence of Eastern Orthodox Churches and the use of Cyrillic script. Their legacy is far more than religious. In the wake of the

brothers, Slavs developed literature and documents of commerce. People of creative talent and business acumen, previously unable to express themselves among peers, found an outlet for communication. Orthodox priests used scripture to teach and found their schools fully subscribed.

United by language, modern nations began to emerge. Forts and monasteries evolved into cultural centers. The change in society begun by Cyril and Methodius cannot be overstated. The brothers are often credited as providing the foundation for Slavic civilization in eastern and south-eastern Europe. In a cruise to ports of the Black Sea, the impact of Cyril and Methodius is strikingly apparent. They will appear in stained glass and statues together in churches, libraries, and town squares of independent, Eastern Orthodox Christian and highly literate nations, of port cities on the Black Sea coast. To know of them is to appreciate and enjoy their continuing legacy.

CONSTANTA, ROMANIA

(ANCIENT TOMIS)

2,000 Years from Ovid to the Casino in Constanta

In the last 2,000 years, the port of Constanta, Romania, has gone from a station of last resort to a resort of choice. When the fifty-year-old Roman poet, Ovid, was banished to Constanta in 10 CE, he regarded the act as worse than a death sentence. The city was then known as Tomis, an ancient Greek settlement. In 10 CE, Tomis was controlled by Rome and regarded as one of its furthermost outposts. The worst insult the emperor could bestow, worse than honorable death, was banishment to Tomis. The depth of insult was not lost on Ovid.

Today visitors to Constanta are greeted by a lovely casino on the water's edge. Built in 1910, and offered for sale to finance refurbishment in 2010, the casino is a postcard icon of Constanta. This is the story of then and now, the story of the bane of Ovid to the beauty of today.

Constanta 10 CE: Expiration of Poetic License

Publius Ovidius Naso, better known as Ovid, was born in 43 BCE, outside of Rome. Rome was the center of his intellectual and poetic world. That he would end his life in 17 CE in Tomis, on the Black Sea coast, at the farthest reach of the Roman world, was an unimaginable end, particularly for a vibrant young man living in Rome in the high point of its existence.

Ovid in Constanta

Ovid was a poet. His poetry consisted largely of love sonnets, which encapsulated mythology and local events. As such, they have become part of the historical record, relied upon by academics for a vision of Roman society just before the beginning of the Christian era. His poetic technique was a model for later poets. The imagery in Ovid's poetry inspired artists of Renaissance Florence to put scenes from Ovid on canvas and in sculpture.

Once Ovid relocated to Tomis, his poems became autobiographical. His descriptions of Tomis are full of self-pity and loathing for the place. The artistic talent did not vanish, but the subject matter was less compelling as examples of the artist's legacy. The poems were of personal pain.

In his youth, Ovid was unapologetically insolent. His affluent family provided a carefree life and good schools to foster development of a man of consequence in Roman society. His father hoped Ovid would become a lawyer, as he showed promise in rhetoric. Instead, Ovid's arguments tended to be emotional. He left school as a teen and traveled to Greece, Sicily, and the east, known as the Levant or Anatolia, that is in western Turkey.[21]

---

[21] Ovid's brother, one year older, may have satisfied their father's desire to have a lawyer in the family, however, the older brother died at twenty-one.

Ovid was recognized for his poetic talent while in his teens. He wrote poems that were erotic and popular. His early work included love odes to absent lovers of well-known heroines. Heroines included goddesses Phyllis, Phaedra, Hypsiple, Ariadne, and Medea. In these letters, Ovid gave personalities to the women. He delved into psycho-social relationships. He was prolific, fascinating, original, and displayed insight into the psyche of women and relationships.[22]

Bowing to the wishes of his father, Ovid put aside poetry for a few years and accepted a position in public administration in Rome. The effort was futile. Ovid's natural inclination was to write from the depth of emotion, not trivial pursuits of politicians. He sought out the most accomplished poets of the great city and enjoyed their friendship. This was the time of Horace and Virgil. Talent as a poet was highly prized in Roman society.

Ovid soon returned to writing poetry, as if he never actually went into hiatus. A separate and weighty compendium of love poems, *Amores*, was eventually edited down to three volumes. All of the poems in the several volumes are written to one woman, Corine. Poems wind through each aspect of a relationship. Poems are written to Corine's hair dying, her dead parrot, and her servant girl, with whom Ovid writes of having an affair. Ovid scholars believe that there was never just one woman, even though the poems are detailed and specifically attributed by Ovid. More likely, Corine is a fictional composite of women in Ovid's life, or of his desires and thoughts of several women expressed to one image of a woman, his Corine.

Ars Amatoria, The Art of Love, is a three-volume manual for women on seduction. Ovid asks readers to tell others that he was their teacher. *Ara Amatoria* was followed closely by *Remedy Amores*, The Cure of Love, written for men. This poem advises men not to be jealous, to take several lovers, and to be spontaneous. All of the volumes on love were written by the time Ovid was forty. One can imagine where he spent time as a young man when not in school.

---

[22] There are also letters between couples, such as Paris and Helen of Troy, attributed to Ovid, but there is controversy on this attribution.

Site of Tomis at the Time of Ovid

Ovid's personal love life was just as active as his poetry writing. He was married three times and divorced twice by the time he was thirty. His third wife was part of a family with some political clout, although not enough to resolve his political problems when they arose. His in-laws were able to support him when he went into exile. The political stature of his in-laws and Ovid's popularity with the public, which made him a highly visible public figure, no doubt weighed on the decision of the emperor to spare Ovid from worse consequences than exile.

By 7 CE, Ovid was fifty-years-old and living in Rome. He was moderately prosperous and, as evidenced in his poetry, a happy man. He was devoted to his wife. She became the object of his love poems. No doubt, many women in Rome wished their husbands could be as expressive. Ovid had patrons in the royal family. Association with the inner circle of the emperor was enjoyed by Ovid as it added to his social standing. Familiarity with royals also contributed to his demise.

In 8 CE, Ovid was banished from Rome to Tomis. The reason for the exile is not known. It is only known that the crime was a serious offense. Whatever it was, the event reflected directly upon the inner family of Roman Emperor Caesar Augustus. Ovid crossed into forbidden turf.

Augustus sent two of his grandchildren into exile at the same time. The husband of one of the grandchildren was given a death sentence for conspiracy against Caesar. As detailed as Ovid's poetry had been on the subject of love, it was always vague when it came to referencing this matter. Augustus was quick and harsh in his judgments. He was the ruler who delivered Rome from civil war. As a result, Rome forgave their emperor for judgments, however severe.

Ovid enjoyed growing up in a peaceful Rome, unscathed by battles with the great Caesar, or of war ineptly fought by Mark Anthony. Although historians have thoroughly searched historical records, none reveal intimate personal thoughts of Augustus as he dealt with palace intrigue, at the heart of which was his granddaughter. Did Augustus fear Ovid's love poems led people astray?

Ovid may have simply seen something that he should not have and had to be sent away. Ovid remarks in poems that his enemies created a more severe situation than his actions deserved. He always believed that those who were jealous of his talent, and of his easy access to all places in society, sought to diminish him. Whatever the offense, there was no pardon. Augustus died three years before Ovid. Successor Emperor Tiberius did not recall Ovid. Ovid lost his life in Rome, his property, contact with his wife and daughter; all that was important to him.

Over the years, scholars have looked for clues to the crime in Ovid's poetry. Some historians have postulated that perhaps the whole affair was fiction. However, the exile was real. If true, it may have been rooted in adultery. There were strict laws in Rome against the adultery promoted in Ovid's poetry. Augustus was the embodiment of moral virtue. In context, Ovid's poems could be construed as treasonous, or, at the least, a poke at the old man on the throne.

The exile interrupted a period of Ovid's work that had shifted from erotic to patriotic. Clearly, by age fifty, Ovid was thinking of his larger legacy. He began writing opus works that encapsulated the entire Roman intellectual world. The Caesar who banished him had been his intended patron, as Ovid wrote books of poetry dedicated to the glory of Rome, in the time of Augustus Caesar. The body of post-banishment work is often referred to as *exile poetry;* odes to forgiveness.[23]

As an example of moving beyond love poetry, Ovid's *Metamorphoses* was a fifteen-book epic effort to catalog Greek and Roman mythology from the beginning of time to Julius Caesar. It is a poetic anthology of 250 myths. Poems run from the creation of man and his world to the flood, and then to the creation of Thebes. There are loves, muses, rivalries, and doomed relationships. Ovid chronicles the actions of Medea, the flight of Daedalus, the exploits of Achilles, and the deification of Caesar. The poem praises Augustus in an unabashed attempt at a showing of loyalty, written just before or during the palace inquest. The *Metamorphoses* is an open bid to immortality for its author. It was barely finished before Ovid was forced to leave Rome.

After *Metamorphoses*, Ovid began *Fasti*. In *Fasti*, Ovid attempted to record all festivals in the Roman astrological calendar, in a six-volume poem. *Fasti* was interrupted by Ovid's departure. He was only able to record the first six months, January to June.

In exile, Ovid's theme changed to self-pity. He imbedded his poetry with an urgent plea to return home. The first poetic effort in exile was *Ibis*, the Ovid, where he cursed the enemies who sent him to Tomis. The *Tristia* was written from 9-12 CE, in which Ovid openly argued for his return to Rome. He learned his poetry was banned in Rome, erasing his memory and depriving his family of income. He then wrote poems as though they were personal letters to friends. These were sad missives to those he loved.

The *Epistulae ex Ponto,* Letters from the Black Sea, is an autobiographical account of how much fun he was not having in Tomis. Ovid wrote of his loneliness and of his disdain for the local barbarians. He wrote love poems to his wife and implored friends to seek his return. He wrote about his needs, his health, and the weather. From Rome, Ovid's enemies were still taunting him.

---

[23] Denis Feeney, introduction to the David Raeburn translation of Metamorphoses, Penguin Books, 2004, at xix.

Ovid shot back in a poem, "where's the joy in stabbing my dead flesh?" In 16 CE, the poems end. In 17 CE Ovid is dead.

Ovid was buried outside of Tomis in a town renamed Ovidiu in his honor. Ovid hated Tomis, but his hosts adored him. He is considered the first Romanian poet, an accolade of high honor. A prominent spot in Constanta is the location of a statue to Ovid's memory. The main square in the city is Ovidiu Square. He is remembered as a victim of his own talent, a person to be revered by those who have known love. As it states in the inscription on the pedestal to his statue, may he rest gently.

National Museum on Ovidiu Square

Constanta 2010 CE and Beyond: Traveler's Choice

Ovid is remembered in Constanta today by the statue of him in the center of old town, Ovid's Square. It is a delightful tribute to a man who openly expressed hatred for his every moment in Constanta. Had he arrived today, his attitude may have been different.

Today Constanta is the third-largest city in Romania. The name was changed, in the fourth century, from ancient Tomis to Constanta. The name changed, accompanying entry of Christianity in Romania, as a tribute to Emperor

Constantine, the first Christian Roman emperor. During the millennium up to the fifteenth century, Byzantine rulers of the Eastern Orthodox Church controlled most of the circumference of the Black Sea.

Constanta was given a Muslim name after the fall of Byzantium in 1453, and during control by the Ottoman Turks. In the nineteenth century, upon dissolution of the Ottoman Empire, the city name reverted to Constanta. Revolving Greek, Roman, Byzantium, Muslim and twentieth-century Communist control, have each left a visible layer of structures in the city.

Today cruise travelers arrive at the water's edge in sight of the Constanta icon, the Casino. The prominent building is a fanciful, art nouveau style creation. It welcomes tourists to promises of fun times, lingering by the building, or walking the surrounding pedestrian area, for a view of the Black Sea, even though the days of a lively gambling den have passed. If Constanta city leaders can muster funds, they will see the Casino reopened as an entertainment venue. For now, the building is the embodiment of dreams; of the past and for the future.

The Casino began construction in 1880, shortly after the demise of the controlling Ottoman Empire in 1877. The city reverted its name to Constanta at that time. For Romania and Constanta, the Casino became emblematic of a change in times and a hope for good fortune. It was important to city leaders that the building make a statement about rebirth of the city.

The initial Casino building was a modest wooden structure. It served as a public meeting place. There was a ballroom and two reading rooms, where tourists could enjoy a newspaper while they gazed at the sea. On summer evenings, there were organized balls, accompanied by a military brass band.[24] In 1891, a strong storm rose up off of the Black Sea and destroyed most of the wood building. It was replaced in 1893 by a wood and brick structure. The ballroom and promenade along the ocean soon returned to use.

Over the next ten years, the city elite of Constanta continually expressed their desire for a grand building at the Casino site, something resembling structures

---

[24] True Romania, The Casino in Constanta, April 2009, http://surprising-romania.blogspot.com/2009/04/casino-in-constan.html. Last visited 6/4/2012.

found on the French Rivera. In 1907, their wish was granted. The thirty-two-year-old Romanian architect, Daniel Renard, a graduate of the School of Fine Arts in Paris, was given a commission to give form to dreams. He did not disappoint. The Art Nouveau style building seen today was completed in 1910.

Within a year of completion of the Casino, the city council authorized gambling. There were seventeen tables for card games and two billiard tables. Almost immediately, Constanta Casino became the preferred gambling destination for the international elite. It became the latest in-spot for those who considered the Riviera too crowded with attention-seekers. Formal attire was always required in all the rooms. This was a place Ovid could appreciate.

The Casino was not universally appreciated in Constanta. Gambling supported by the city governors offended Muslims in the city. Ottoman Turks had ceded political control, but after four hundred years of being a part of the Ottoman

Empire, Constanta was still a city where Muslims constituted a significant part of the population. When the historic Romanian population took control of the city and national leadership, they remained a minority in numbers.

King Carol I of Romania rose to resolve city tensions by offering royal funds to build a new mosque. Also completed in 1910, was the Great Mosque, prominently placed on Ovid Square. Gambling continued in the Casino until it was closed during World War I. Debates on gambling at the Casino persisted in the Romanian Parliament during the war-time hiatus.

During World War I, the Casino became a hospital for the troops. The building suffered extensive damage from bombs. After the war, it was returned to its full glory. By 1914, the Casino was grand enough to provide a venue for the Romanian Royal family to host a ball for the Russian royal family. The royal era was short-lived.

Home of Romanian Royals in Constanta 1881 to 1914

Grand Duchess Olga of Russia was not impressed with efforts of the Romanian royal family to show themselves worthy of a Russian royal union. She refused Prince Carol's proposal of marriage. The Russians' scorning of Romanian royals caused a major scandal. The Russian entourage sailed home from Constanta, leaving the Prince holding the ball, so to speak. Shortly after sailing home , the Russian royal family was imprisoned and shot by Bolsheviks. The communist era blanketed ethnic tensions within controlled countries and ended frivolous pursuits such as gambling.

After World War II, the Casino suffered from neglect. Funds for recreation and enjoyment of the proletariat was not a priority of the Communist government. Lavish spending on Central Party members was undertaken in remote, exclusive resorts, while venues such as the Casino were touted as excesses of the imperial era, to be disparaged. In 1985, elegant old casino furnishings were replaced with pedestrian, functional pieces, rather than restore prior glory.

Upon the demise of the Soviet Union, the Casino reverted to local government control. In 2007, the public building was leased to a private company, with the hope the Casino could reopen with private funds. Nothing came of the effort. As the Casino hit the century mark, it was offered for sale. It remained closed, while interested investors contemplated expense of restoration.

Despite being closed, the Casino drew people to its promenade along the Black Sea. It became an icon of the city, making restoration of the interior and preservation of the exterior important. Along the promenade, with the Casino as a backdrop, artists and craft sellers set up tents to engage visitors to Constanta. Resurgence of tourism will mandate a renewed chapter of fun times in the Casino. The spirit of Ovid remains on the main square of Constanta, waiting to give a thumbs up to what Constanta can become as an attractive diversion from Rome.

Constanta Casino Awaiting Renewal on Promenade

ODESSA, UKRAINE

(ANCIENT OLBIA)

Ribas and Richelieu Remake Russia

Compared to other ports of the Black Sea, Odessa in history is a short story. The ancient port site of Olbia was abandoned a millennium before the present city was founded.[25] The new city was conceived as a monument to new Russia, in the second half of the eighteenth century by the famous lover of Catherine the Great, Grigori Aleksandrovich Potemkin.[26] The most famous landmark of the city, its entrance stairway, is named for this one-eyed visionary.[27]

Potemkin was devoted to Catherine. His most opulent gift to her is the famous golden Peacock Clock, forever encased in glass in her boudoir in the Hermitage in St. Petersburg. Catherine returned the emotion, referring to Potemkin as her husband. Her gift to him is a palace outside St. Petersburg. Their joint triumph is seen in Odessa.

In 1794, when Catherine proclaimed the site of the new city, she named an Italian-born Spaniard and Russian military hero, José Pascual Domingo de Ribas y Boyons, as its first administrator. De Ribas is credited with choosing to name the city after the powerful Greek god, Odysseus. He displayed his

---

25   Neal Ascherson, Black Sea, Hill and Wang, New York, 1995, p. 74.

26   Catherine was 44 when the 34-year-old Potemkin became her lover. He was devoted to her, was educated and a capable administrator. Ian Grey, Catherine the Great: Autocrat and Empress of all Russia, Hodder and Stoughton, London, 1961, pp. 170-176.

27   The loss of an eye was not the result of a military skirmish, but more likely a quarrel between lovers of Catherine. Historians record fights as between Potemkin and Grigori Orlov, the father of Catherine's son. Charles King, Odessa: Genius and Death in a City of Dreams, W.W. Norton & Company, New York, 2011, p. 39.

well-regarded tact and good judgment in relenting to the feminine moniker of Odessa, in recognition of the female patron monarch. José de Ribas, better known to Odessans as Deribas, did not live to see his plans come to fruition. The main city hub of Deribasovskaya Street honors his memory.

The man who brought Odessa to life was a Frenchman in exile, Armand, the Duc de Richelieu. His accomplishments would have made his great-uncle, the Cardinal, proud. This Richelieu built the city, kept it alive during successive plagues, and established it as a center of trade and culture.

Together, non-Russians Ribas and Richelieu remade the image of Russia to give Catherine the Great what she most wanted, a signature city. Development of Odessa was demonstrative proof that Russia could be as cultured as any leading capital of Europe in its day. Over the next two hundred years, fortunes of Odessa mirrored major events in world history. Today the visitor will enjoy what was envisioned as a tourist delight. Ribas and Richelieu welcome visitors to Catherine's Black Sea gateway city, the perennial resort city of Ukraine.

Spanish-Italian Designs for a Russian City

Catherine had good reason to often rely on Potemkin for advice. Under his military command, she expanded boundaries of her domain to include Novorossiya, New Russia, which we now know as Ukraine. He then encouraged Germans and other disaffected souls to settle and farm there. The newcomers were under the watch of equally disaffected Russian aristocrats, who were given tracts of land in the newly acquired region. Everyone seemed pleased. At least temporarily.

To delight Catherine with all that he had created for her, Potemkin arranged a tour for her to the south lands. Of course, not much had actually been created, except political control. Instead, Potemkin staged a grand show along the route of Catherine's entourage of two hundred carriages and sleds. Townspeople waved at her from mock front village markets. There were parades along the route. At one point, as the entourage came around a mountain, they were treated to a view of a mock Vesuvius, that was actually a trench cut in a mountain, filled with a flammable liquid and torched at the crescendo moment. These towns became known as *Potemkin Villages*.[28]

When in 1787, the Ottomans threatened to expand their empire and infringe on Catherine's domain, Potemkin advised her on military leaders.[29] One choice was not memorable, but another appointment had long-standing positive consequences. The disappointing choice was a man well known to Americans as a distinguished hero of the American War of Independence, John Paul Jones. The choice with lasting star quality was de Ribas, junior aide to Jones.

As a mercenary for the young country with no navy, Jones maneuvered his small ships around the British to claim victories for the Americans. As a

---

[28] There were no hotels in which Catherine could lodge, so Potemkin cleaned up the aging Bakhchisarai Palace, 14th century home of the Khans. Guests delighted in sleeping in former rooms of the harem or of the Great Khan. Catherine preserved this landmark, when she later tore down other historical sites to build her new city. Charles King, The Black Sea, A History, Oxford, Oxford, 2004.

[29] It was Catherine's belief that all the Ottomans brought to Russia was the plague each fall. King, Odessa, p. 45.

mercenary for the Russians, Jones was not as successful. He was not familiar with Russian vessels, tactical advantages to be taken in the shallows of the port area, or the ways of war in the Black Sea. The Russian practice of driving an enemy ship to a shallow area and then fire-bombing the stranded vessel, seemed unsporting to Jones. He left the Black Sea for St. Petersburg, with its warmer quarters. Jones left Russia after a scandal and eventually died in Paris in 1792.[30]

Russian Street Signs and French Architecture in Odessa

---

[30] The scandal involved accusations of rape of a twelve-year-old girl. Jones claimed it was consensual and that he had not been her first lover. King, The Black Sea, A History, p. 160. Views of Jones and his actions in Russia depend on the historian. Some claim that Jones was indecisive in battle with the Ottomans, or was intimidated by them. Others write that the Greek and English-trained Russian generals wished to be in charge and command victories for their tsar, so they ignored orders given by Jones, or sidelined his participation. Samuel Eliot Morison, John Paul Jones: A Sailor's Biography, Little Brown & Company, Boston, 1959, pp. 360-390. There is no doubt that war in the Black Sea was a place in which Jones did not fit.

Odessa Opera House

José de Ribas had been a Russian court liaison since 1772, and knew the internal politics of Potemkin's administration. He was well-schooled as a politician, born in 1749, in Naples, as the son of Spain's counsel to Italy and his Irish wife. With his mixed heritage and education, de Ribas was emblematic of residents of Black Sea ports. He was a Christian, European, who spoke the language of Italian merchant seamen. He was also a shrewd tactician, whose ambition it was to break from the stifling structure of classical cities of Italy and Spain, to be part of something new.

Jones was never given rank higher than rear admiral, whereas his lieutenant, de Ribas, attained the rank of admiral by the end of the Ottoman conflict. Potemkin praised Ribas for his compassion in dealing with drunken sailors, with firm talk instead of harsh punishment. When de Ribas utilized a small Russian contingent to take control of an Ottoman held fort at Khadjibey, he was memorialized in Lord Byron's poem, *Don Juan.* Of all of his career achievements, the best contribution made by de Ribas was the recognition that the small fort at Khadjibey sat at a strategic point on the Black Sea, from which entrance to the Danube, Dniester, Dnieper and Bug rivers could be controlled. That strategic point was also a potential trade hub. The fort site became Odessa.

Catherine proclaimed the development of a new city to begin at the site chosen by de Ribas. She appointed him city administrator in 1794. Two years later, Catherine was dead. Her son Paul took no interest in any of his mother's plans. By the time Paul was removed in a palace coup, de Ribas was also dead. He did not live to see his genius in selecting the site of Odessa to come to fruition.

At the beginning of the nineteenth century, Napoleon moved through Europe, in his military conquest to control European commerce. As part of his strategy, Napoleon placed a ban on Hungarian wheat shipments. Instantly, Odessa became important as the center of trade, feeding Europe. Grain and cowhide from the Russian Steppes, along with olive oil and dried fruit and nuts from the Middle East, moved west and north into starving Europe. Italian goods left Europe and were sent throughout the eastern world through Odessa. The little fort town, the dream city of Ribas, had the funds from trade to enable building a major city.

French Odessa

Ribas on a Backstreet in Odessa

French Servant to Nobility Builds the Russian Center of World Commerce

Richelieu as born in 1766, with the life of a French courtier guaranteed to him. He was only twenty when he inherited his grandfather's position as First Gentleman of the King's Bedchamber to French King Louis. Although imbued with life among the royals, and a confidant to Marie Antoinette, Richelieu was savvy to changes taking place in France. He advised Marie Antoinette not to return to Paris, while he escaped to Russia. To her peril, she did not take his advice.

In 1803, at the age of only thirty-seven, Richelieu was appointed by Tsar Alexander I to be chief city administrator of Odessa. At a time when fellow Frenchman, Pierre Charles L'Enfant, was turning a swamp area on the Potomac River into the American nation's capital, Richelieu was turning designs he inherited from de Ribas into a modern port city.[31] Much like Washington, in the United States, Odessa street plans were in sharp contrast to mud clogged paths where throngs of carts created deep ruts in streets, from which peddlers and farmers sold their goods.

In eleven years, from 1803 to 1814, Richelieu oversaw construction of several large public administrative buildings, public schools, a library, and a theater. One of the public buildings housed the printing press and the most important bureaucrat, the state censor. In Odessa, books and pamphlets were published in several languages, reflective of the multinational population of the city. As an indication of the large Italian population of Odessa, the result of hundreds of years of an impact of Genoese and Venetian shippers, street signs were printed in Italian and Russian.

Richelieu put his mark on city infrastructure, such as boulevards, with large medians planted with trees. Nearby residents were given responsibility to water the plants. The harbor was expanded to hold one hundred and fifty sailing ships.

---

[31] Washington, DC was founded in 1790. Buildings on the streetscape of L'Enfant began around 1800.

As the city grew to a population of 35,000, its residents became increasingly conscious of their living conditions. People enhanced private property and built lovely homes. They paid for carriages to take them to the theater, rather than walk through mud in yet unpaved streets. Richelieu instituted banking systems and commercial courts to support rapid economic growth.

Nothing could protect the beautiful new city from the larger environment in which it existed. Just as Catherine the Great had complained, every fall, ships that brought goods from Turkish ports also brought disease. Beautiful Odessa was not immune to plague.

Saving the City

Sequestering incoming cargo to protect from unwanted traveling fleas carrying disease, was a concept well-known in nineteenth-century Odessa. Although the cause of disease was not understood, containing the vector was. Venice and Dubrovnik had in prior centuries instituted systems of containment of goods and travelers for the detection of disease before entry. Richelieu instituted the best-known systems of his time. He built a quarantine facility down from the harbor, in which incoming goods were fumigated for fleas. Travelers were inspected for signs of disease. At any hint of trouble, travelers were held until any possibility of disease was resolved.

Even the best system for disease control could be penetrated by wealth and privilege. In August 1812, a wealthy ship's passenger brought a beautiful gold ring to his favorite actress in the Odessa theater. The jewelry was wrapped in cotton within its case. Hiding in the cotton were fleas. Within thirty-six hours of receiving the gift, the actress was dead. Soon after that, other actors in the theater company and their servants were ill and dying. Catherine's scourge of the Ottomans was running rampant through Odessa.

Richelieu quickly acted. He closed down all public buildings, including churches and theaters. He brought together all the city doctors and assigned them sectors of the city to patrol for the disease. By November 12, various city neighborhoods were quarantined. Troops were recalled from fighting against the advance of Napoleon in Russia to enforce curfews and quarantines.

Prisoners of the city jail were put into service loading carts with the dead to be quickly buried. The cart bearers wore oil-soaked cloaks to protect from fleas and the spread of disease. On every street, fires were burning to smoke out fleas. As mass graves were dug for bodies to be burned, Richelieu could be seen picking up a shovel to assist the fatigued grave diggers, as every hand was employed to save the city.[32]

Between August 12, 1812, and January 13, 1813, death from plague claimed ten percent of the city population, which was about 2,700 people. But for the actions of Richelieu, the toll would have been much higher. The winter of 1813 was severe and helped to kill remaining fleas. The winter cold also kept people indoors, where they curtailed spread of fleas in winter wool and fur coats. By the fall of 1813, the trauma of the prior fall was a dimming memory. One legacy of the prior winter was a record high birthrate by the fall of 1813.

Richelieu Greets Visitors to Odessa Today

32   King, Odessa, p. 64.

Unlike his predecessors in Russia and Europe, Richelieu did not blame the Jews for the plague. Instead, he had an intellectual response. Jews in Odessa, although blame-free, continued to be treated at separate hospitals as they had before the events of 1812.

In 1814, King Louis XVIII replaced Napoleon as head of France. Odessa was made a tax-free port. Richelieu packed a single small case with a few clean shirts and departed Odessa to become the Prime Minister of France. He died in France in 1822, just before he turned sixty. At the time of his death, his world was at peace. In 1828, a statue of Richelieu, wearing classical Greek garb, was installed on a bluff overlooking the harbor at a location that became the top of the *Potemkin Steps*,[33] between the harbor and Deribasovskaya Street. It is Richelieu who greets cruise passengers as they arrive in the port of Odessa. The statue to Catherine sits further inland, in a traffic circle. The statue to Ribas is at the end of a small side street. Richelieu is ever vigilant against harmful pests invading the city.

Catherine the Great Traffic Circle Odessa

---

[33] Construction of the Odessa landmark, the 220 steps, 192 remaining, was overseen by Richelieu's successor, Vorontsov, from 1837 to 1841, designed by Italian architect Francesco Boffo, but that is another story. See: Pushkin in Odessa, also Itinerary IV. The steps derived their name from the 1925 film, *The Battleship Potemkin*. Before the film they were the Primorsky Stairs.

Odessa: Movie Set or Stage to History

Potemkin Steps with Richelieu at the Top

In 1905, there was no massacre on the Potemkin Steps. The event and its location are remembered over time as fact, although the whole incident was a figment of creative cinema. In 1925, Stalin commissioned Soviet silent filmmaker, Sergei Eisenstein, to transform Odessa from an imperial city to the birthplace of the Soviet Union. The historic film he created was *The Battleship Potemkin*, a fictional account of a Tsarist massacre of revolutionaries.

The period of 1904 to 1912, was a time of great political upheaval in Russia as it moved from aristocracy to communism. In 1905, the real-life royal battleship *Potemkin* was seized by revolutionaries. For months, the ship traveled the Black Sea, terrorizing shippers until the crew decided to surrender in the port city of

Constanta, Romania.[34] Some of the crew remained in Romania and went on with their lives, while others were returned to Russia, where they were hanged as traitors.

In the film, there is a scene where citizens of Odessa lay massacred on the steps. In the middle of the steps, a baby carriage comes slowly down from the top. There is an infant in the carriage, who survives. Thus, the new Russia, the allegory of that baby, is born from tragedy. As an additional dramatic effect, there are stone lions on the steps, which rise, as does Russia.[35]

The film premiered in Odessa in 1925. It was seen by Douglas Fairbanks and Mary Pickford, who brought it to the United States.[36] City scenes were actually shot in Riga, home of the film producer.[37]

Today the visitor to Odessa will see a statue of Catherine II, the Great, of Russia, the patron of Odessa. The statue was removed early in the twentieth century by Bolsheviks, who replaced it with a bust of Karl Marx. The Marx statue was removed by the Soviets for a statue of a hero of the Potemkin mutiny. Eventually, Catherine was returned to her prime spot in the city center. Odessa has traveled through tumultuous times to regain its stature as the city of de Ribas and Richelieu, for the visitor's pleasure. It exists today as the beautiful port city, as they intended.

---

[34] Bernard Pares, A History of Russia, Dorset Press, New York, 1953, pp. 450-451.

[35] The lions can be seen at the Vorontsov summer palace in the Crimea, but that is another story.

[36] King, Odessa, p. 194.

[37] See Cruise through History Itinerary XI Ports of the Baltic, Port of Riga, for the further story of the father, architect of Riga, and son the film producer.

PUSHKIN'S ODESSA

Pushkin was a Russian icon. He would have appreciated the play of words. In his youth, he enjoyed being irresponsible. He was prolific in writing fanciful poetry. By his twenties, Pushkin wanted to be taken seriously and compared to Lord Byron, the well-traveled English poet. Pushkin wrote odes, much in the style of Byron, to be published in books, first for the fame of it and secondarily for the income.

As he neared thirty, Aleksandr Pushkin decided he should marry. He never settled down. He did marry a beautiful young woman, they had four children, and he attempted to take over his family's estate. Pushkin also turned from poet to historian. He wrote histories of the rise of serfs, which garnered him immediate disdain from critics and a long-term place of honor in Marxist and Soviet Russia. By age thirty-eight, Pushkin was dead.

This is the short story of the short life of Aleksandr Pushkin and of his brief time in Odessa. Time spent in Odessa was only about two years, 1823 through 1824. Those years were colorful and emblematic of the turbulent short life of the poet.

Pushkin thought of himself as a latter-day Ovid, the Roman poet banished to Constanta in 8 CE, for being outspoken.[38] Pushkin was exiled to the Crimea in 1820, where there was no social life for the poet. He eventually obtained a position on the staff of Mikhail Vorontsov, who, in 1823, became a successor to Richelieu as chief administrator of Odessa. Pushkin repaid Voronstov's

---

[38] Ovid was aged fifty when he was banished from Rome to Tomis, now Constanta. He hopped a ship from there to the Crimea.

hospitality by engaging in an affair with his host's wife. By the time he was required to leave Odessa, Pushkin was sad to go. Odessa was a European styled Russian city.

Pushkin on top the pillar at the end of Primorsky Boulevard in Pushkin Square, Odessa

Life Before Odessa

Aleksandr Pushkin was born in Moscow in 1799. A biographer notes that he was born in a half-brick and half-timber house.[39] He was also born into a family that was half nobility and half former slave. Pushkin's father's family was descendant of Russian nobility, although his father was an idle businessman, who dissipated his inherited assets. Pushkin's maternal great-grandfather was

---

[39]   T.J. Binyon, Pushkin: A Biography, Alfred A. Knopf, New York, 2003.

a black African of noble birth, who was brought as a slave to the estate of Peter the Great. This man was Abram Gannibal, a favorite of Tsar Peter, who ended his life as a general.

Gannibal's daughter was introduced into St. Petersburg society, a legacy she shared with her daughter, Nadezhda. Nadezhda, Pushkin's mother, was fluent in French and well educated. Neither parent gave Aleksandr much attention. He spent his youth on the estate of his maternal grandmother, an estate of 2,500 acres, thirty miles outside of Moscow, attended to by sixty serfs.

Although Pushkin considered his grandmother's estate to be *back behind nowhere*, this is the home he returned to from St. Petersburg and Odessa when he needed a place of refuge. At the end of his life, Pushkin was able to preserve the estate for his children. He wrote poems there, but none inspired by the grand place it must have been.

Young Pushkin was an avid reader from an early age. In his father's and grandmother's homes, he was exposed to published poets and authors. A distant relative had translated Moliére.[40] His uncle Vasily wrote a poem too risqué to be published. It was this uncle who took young Aleksandr to St. Petersburg to begin school at the royal Lycée, in 1811. Separated from family, the school became his home. Pushkin was noted by his schoolmaster to be more talented than diligent in studies. He was known as someone always available for a party.

Pushkin began writing poems at age thirteen. He first published in a local paper at fourteen, to attract the attention of a young girl. By the time Pushkin finished school at seventeen, he was known broadly for his poetry and for his love of women. Recognized Russian poets identified Pushkin as a leading artist. The Hussar soldiers whom he wished to emulate observed Pushkin's devotions to gods Bacchus and Venus. Bacchus for his ability to consume alcohol and Venus for his adoration of women. However, when forced to choose an occupation, the young poet chose civil service.

In 1817, Pushkin was sworn into the civil service of Tsar Alexander I in St. Petersburg. He enjoyed roaming the streets in a long black coat and stove-pipe

---

[40]   Binyon, p. 13.

hat, with dirty fingernails. Hardly the garb of an aristocrat. He rarely showed up for work, although it provided him with an income. His poems written at this time were political satires of the Russian government, such as *Fairy Tales*. Aleksandr considered the verse as nothing more than caricature, not insurrection. That was before the 1820s and the Decembrist conspiracy.

The Decembrists were a group of young intellectual revolutionaries bent on overthrowing the monarchy. Although Pushkin was not known to be part of the group, he did admit to meeting with some of them. They were his acquaintances and intellectual sparring partners. Fortunately for Pushkin, as the military unwound the conspiracy and interrogated those held in jail, it became apparent that Pushkin was held outside the organization in the opinion of its central rulers.

The Decembrists confessed that they liked Pushkin, but they would never trust him with a secret. He wrote verses that became rallying songs, but he was considered too frivolous to be relied upon. As a result, Pushkin was exiled by the Tsar, rather than jailed. He could have been sent to Siberia. Out of respect for his talent, Pushkin was sent south to Crimea. Hence the comparison to Ovid.

European Odessa

Monument to the Arts in Odessa at the opposite end of Primorsky Boulevard

On his travels south, Pushkin stayed with an old friend in Kiev. The friend had distinguished himself in the military, and to him, Pushkin dedicated the poem, *The Prisoner of the Caucasus.* Later in the trip, Pushkin was lodging in an old cabin on the Dnieper River when he observed two prisoners, shackled together and chased by guards, as they swam across the river to freedom. He began to write *The Robber Brothers.* Prisoner was published about a year later. It was a fifty-three-page book costing five rubles.

Pushkin's strength was in writing witty short poems of the moment, tributes to women, and current events. His preference was to write substantial odes, in the style of Lord Byron. Long poems garnered higher royalty fees. Pushkin was perennially short of funds. Long poems of substance also garnered high praise and lasting adoration, both of which Pushkin craved in endless amounts.

When not writing poems, or pursuing women, Pushkin was sick with a fever or other ailments. Beyond his reputation for throwing tantrums, was a

Odessa Cathedral – Place of Vorontsov Family Tombs

history of minor illness, unusually frequent for such a young man. Pushkin considered himself the victim of the treachery of men and the deceit of women, contributing to his demise. Nothing of consequence was ever his fault or responsibility. To Pushkin, praise received was duly earned and criticism the mistake of others.

For the first three years of his exile, Pushkin lived just outside of Odessa in Kishinev. In this town of 20,000, there were numerous wives and daughters of military men, who left their women in need of company. Pushkin made his way through Kishinev society, one wife or daughter at a time.

For a brief period in 1821, life in Kishinev became exciting. Pushkin had the opportunity to meet Alexander Ypsilanti a year earlier when the Greek freedom campaigner came to Russia in hopes that the Christian tsar would aid the Greeks in liberation from the Ottoman Turks. Now Ypsilanti was fresh from the scene of a massacre of Turks, near a Turkish garrison on the Danube, and heading north.

In the wake of Ypsilanti's travels, Greek refugees came to Kishinev. Everyone in town was talking about whether Alexander I would support their effort. Pushkin became enthralled with a young Greek woman, who he fantasized had a prior relationship with Byron, when the older poet was in Greece. Pushkin's relationship with the woman, Calypso, made him feel closer to Byron. It also gave him a vicarious connection to the freedom fighters. His illusions are unsupported in fact.

On May 9, 1823, exactly three years into his Crimean exile, Pushkin began to write *Eugene Onegin*. At the same time, his military overseer and tour guide through the Crimea was replaced by Count Mikhail Vorontsov. Pushkin was headed to Odessa with Vorontsov.

Trials of a Later Day Ovid in Odessa

Prince Mikhail Semyonovich Vorontsov was born in 1782. He was a Russian aristocrat, son of an ambassador to England for Catherine the Great, raised in London and educated at Cambridge. As a soldier, he attained the rank of major general. His lasting contribution to the military was seeking education for troops. In 1819, when he was twenty-six, Vorontsov married Elizaveta "Lise" Branicka, a grandniece of Potemkin. In 1823, Vorontsov was made the chief officer of Odessa and principle overseer of Pushkin. The latter was the more difficult task.

When he arrived in Odessa, Vorontsov began to build a palace, which still stands at the end of Nikolaeksky Boulevard, also known as Primorsky Boulevard, ironically at the opposite end of the treed walkway from what is now Pushkin Plaza, anchored by the obelisk to Pushkin. Incorporated within the Odessa palace of Vorontsov are architectural pieces from the Mikhailovsky Palace in St. Petersburg. The old palace was the residence of Paul I, son of Catherine, and the location of his murder.[41] Included in the Odessa residence is a Turkish

---

[41]   Prince Vorontsov was advisor to Tsar Paul I, his father was an ambassador to England for Paul's mother, Catherine II, Catherine the Great, and his great uncle Count Vorontsov, builder of the family mansion in St. Petersburg, was advisor to Paul's

Vorontsov Palace and Pushkin Guest Home in Odessa

Chamber, a place for sumptuous parties given by Vorontsov's wife, Lise. The Vorontsov Odessa palace was under construction from 1823 until 1830. Until that time, Lise had to make do with parties given in various, less glamorus, local settings.

When Pushkin arrived in Odessa, he made a point of meeting the women of society, married and single, older and younger than he. He frequented the city's dark side and was always on the prowl for a party. It was inevitable that, as Vorontsov was busy with affairs of the city and building his new home, Lise and Pushkin would strike up an amorous relationship.

As long as the affair of his wife and his ward was discrete, Vorontsov had few complaints. After all, Vorontsov had a mistress, Olga, ten years his junior.

---

father Tsar, Peter III. See more on the family Vorontsov and the home of Prince Vorontsov in Yalta.

However, Pushkin was always desirous of being indiscrete. He was open about the affair and wrote poems praising Lise for her charms and castigating Vorontsov for his dour demeanor. In desperation, Vorontsov wrote to the Russian foreign minister, "Deliver me from Pushkin."[42]

Of Vorontsov, Pushkin wrote that he was half an English lord, half a merchant and sage, and half an ignoramus. Of the halves of personality, Puskin wrote that there was hope Voronstov would be a full of each in the end.[43] Puskin wrote openly with impunity that Voronstov was unable to stem.

In 1824, an opportunity arose for Vorontsov to put Pushkin to work in the cause of the city. An enormous black cloud of locusts descended upon Odessa. Residents built fires in the streets and organized noisy parades to chase away the pests. Vorontsov sent Pushkin into rural areas to assess the locust population, count locust eggs, and send back a report. Instead, Pushkin wrote a little poem, sent it to Vorontsov and resigned. Vorontsov petitioned the tsar, and Pushkin was allowed to leave.

Vorontsov and the tsar had more to be concerned with than Pushkin's affair with Lise. At this time, Odessa was thought to be a Russian outpost infiltrated with Greek patriots and free thinkers. The new tsar, Nicholas I, was concerned that Greek nationalism could fuel ambitions of the Decembrists in any venue that fostered free thought. Pushkin was associated with free thought, so it was time to send him home.[44]

On August 1, 1824, Pushkin was sent home to the family estate. The night before he left, there was one more tryst with Lise. At that time, she gave Pushkin an antique seal ring that had belonged to a Rabbi. It was inscribed with a Hebrew saying. Pushkin wore that ring every day for the remainder of his life. Nine months later, Lise gave birth to a daughter, Sophie.

---

[42] Charles King, Odessa, Genius and Death in a City of Dreams, W.W. Norton and Company, New York, 2011, p. 85.

[43] Binyon, at 173.

[44] When Pushkin's uncle learned of his dismissal, he remarked in an obvious double meaning, "The locusts have got him sacked!" Binyon, at 187.

Postscript to Pushkin in Odessa

Port of Odessa Today

Upon the death of Alexander I, Nicholas I stepped over other likely contenders to take the throne. The Decembrists took the opportunity in uncertain times to incite open rebellion of the Nicholas court. Nicholas retaliated with prosecution and hanging of any quickly convicted conspirators.

Meanwhile, in a show of loyalty to Nicholas, Vorontsov and Lise held a lavish party in his honor in Odessa. While a band played, men in armor marched on the beach, under Chinese lanterns. Mademoiselle Mariconi of the Odessa Opera was rowed ashore while singing a Rossini aria. Nicholas was impressed.[45]

---

[45]   King, p. 93.

Vorontsov's legacy in Odessa included opening the Odessa Herald newspaper and a public library in 1830. By the 1840s, there were over one hundred public schools, with four hundred teachers, for five thousand students. Boys and girls were given an education. There were also private schools sanctioned in the Greek, German, Jewish and Armenian communities, as a testament to the diversity of the Odessa population and religious toleration of Vorontsov.

Vorontsov left Odessa in 1845. His crowning achievement in 1841, was opening the two hundred and twenty steps to the port. Critics thought the steps, with ten landings, would collapse. Vorontsov was charged with overspending eight-hundred-thousand rubles for the cost of the endeavor. As a lasting tribute to Vorontsov, the monument to the city has stood over time.

The original sandstone steps have been encased in granite. The ten lowest steps were lost in an expansion of the harbor; otherwise, the original effort remains. Today the steps are a symbol of upward-facing Odessa. At the top of the steps, Richelieu extends his welcoming arm to visitors. By rights, the steps should be called the Vorontsov steps. They are not. They are known as the Potemkin Stairs, in ode to the man who brought Catherine the Great South. At least they are not named Pushkin Steps.

During the Stalin era, Vorontsov Palace became offices of the Communist Children's League, the Young Pioneers. In August 1941, it became the offices of Professor Gheorghe Alexianu, the Nazi governor for Romania. It was here that Odessa residents were registered to determine whether they were Jewish, or a new arrival. In 2005, the home was refurbished. Vorontsov family graves were relocated to the refurbished Spaso-Preobrazhensky Cathedral.

As to Pushkin, he left Odessa at age twenty-six, and died on January 27, 1837, at age thirty-eight, in the aftermath of a duel.[46] In the intervening twelve years, he published some of the work for which he is best known.

---

[46] Some historians believe that after all of Pushkin's carousing and threatening others with duels over insignificant arguments, it was a professional dueler who insulted Pushkin's wife's virtue and prompted the duel that took his life. Bernard Pares, A History of Russia, Dorset Press, New York, 1953:1991, p. 343. Other biographers believe Pushkin's opponent was in love with Natalya, Pushkin's young wife, whom he married after leaving Odessa, and that jealousy clouded Pushkin's thinking. Had Pushkin not perished in a duel he was headed for difficult last days. Nicholas I once

Inspired by meeting Tsar Nicholas I in 1826, Pushkin wrote *The Prophet*, based on biblical Isaiah. In 1830, the historical tragedy *Boris Godunov*, was well-received, likely written on his mother's estate upon return from exile in 1825. Parts of the tale were entrusted to Pushkin's agent, who allowed it to be plagiarized before publication. The poem was made into a ballet, giving the poet greater fame.

The autobiographical, epic travels of *Eugene Onegin*, was written over a long period and published in 1833 when Pushkin was strapped for cash. The poem is regarded as documenting the historical evolution of Russian literary taste. Pushkin then turned historian and wrote of Russian peasant revolts. His masterpiece short story, *The Bronze Horseman*, was written quickly in 1833.

Overall, Pushkin's verse was, at times, critical of the ruling class and at times adoring of them. In popular regard, he was thought of as a dissident and fighter for liberty. Writers suffered repression during the reign of Nicolas I. Even some of Pushkin's light verse could not pass censorship and be published. In the Soviet era, Pushkin was exalted as anti-autocracy and as a historian of the working classes. Regardless of the politics of the day, Russians have always honored Pushkin's work, even if they prefer the man glorified in myth, rather than look too closely at his not-so-private life.

In death, Pushkin received the two things he craved most in life: massive adoration and brisk sales of his work. Upon news of Pushkin's death, about ten thousand visitors paid their respects in two days. In three days, enough copies of Pushkin's published works were purchased to liquidate his debts. Nicholas I forgave debts on Pushkin's mother's estate, his legacy to the four Pushkin children.

The Tsar also granted pensions to Pushkin's wife and to his two daughters until marriage. The two sons were granted pensions and education until they entered royal service as pages. Tsar Nicholas remained a protector of Pushkin's widow and sponsored her marriage to an officer in 1844. She died in St. Petersburg in 1863.

---

noted that when he met Pushkin in 1826, the young poet was quite ill and covered with sores, now known to be signs of syphilis. Binyon, p. 235.

Today in Odessa, people stroll down the pedestrian walkway, Primorsky Boulevard, shaded by trees until the corridor opens to Pushkin Square. At the entrance to the square is an obelisk on which a bust of Pushkin is fixed under the shade of trees. Behind the statue are cannons. Locusts may nibble the flowers in the garden that surrounds the obelisk, although the cannons are unnecessary. Pushkin never saw more active service than entertaining the wives and daughters of soldiers. His poetry is adored by Russians for its spunk and passion.

SEVASTOPOL, UKRAINE

CHERSONESOS AT THE CENTER OF THE WORLD

For two thousand years, the city of Chersonesos commanded a pivotal point in world events. This city on an outcropping of the Crimean Peninsula, on the north shore of the Black Sea, was at the center of the most important matters of the day. Mighty Athens relied upon the city to feed its bulging population from the fifth century BCE, until Rome became beneficiary of Chersonesos exports. In the Christian era, Chersonesos evolved from a trade center to be the exporter of Christianity to the north and throughout Russia.

Chersonesites prized their democratic governance above everything else. Citizens controlled all public functions, including trade agreements and the allocation of farmland, rather than a king, or a few wealthy merchants. Each year, every citizen took an oath to defend democracy and the exports of Chersonesos.

Citizens of Chersonesos felt so strongly about democracy that they avoided forming a military to enforce city rules. As a result, there was no military to protect the city when jealous neighbors threatened their lifestyle. By the second century BCE, it was necessary to sacrifice democracy to obtain protection from nearby kings for the trade port. During its second millennium, Chersonesos was restored by Byzantine emperors and found a new life as a center of Christianity. Byzantium fell in 1453, bringing down the fortunes of Chersonesos. When Tatar hordes came across the Crimea, the city was overwhelmed. Invaders left Chersonesos in ruins.

By the nineteenth century CE, a monastery and church were all that still thrived at the site of the once-great city of Chersonesos. Archaeological excavation began slowly in the nineteenth century and then continued, with short interruptions, for the next one hundred years. Under the rubble, the life story of a former glory was revealed.

For over five hundred years, two cities sat side by side; the modern growing naval port of Sevastopol and the vanquished city down the beach and across the harbor. This is the story of the birth, growth, and resurgence of Chersonesos, the fascinating archaeological site of a city, which was in its day at the center of the world. Today Sevastopol is awakened to its neighbor and welcomes visitors to Chersonesos.

Founding a Democratic City in the Crimea

Chersonesos was founded in 422 BCE, several centuries later than Greek colonies on the southern shores of the Black Sea.[47] The founding inhabitants were Greeks, who came across the Black Sea from Herakleia Pontica, another of the colonies sponsored by the town of Megara, north of Athens. In the fifth century BCE, there was nothing new about Greeks colonizing shores of the Black Sea. They had been doing so for four hundred years before founding Chersonesos. Greek travel to the area and desire to control the Black Sea region went back to 1200 BCE, the time of the battle at Troy and Jason and the Argonauts.

The force that stymied settlement for Greeks was gaining entrance to the Black Sea. The Hellespont was closed to them until the eighth century BCE. Before that time, Phœnicians, Assyrians and Miletus, the power city south of Ephesus in Turkey, controlled the Dardanelles, the access to the Black Sea. The Trojan War, a lovely story of love lost and retaken, may have actually been a battle over access to the Black Sea.

---

[47] There are no graves at Chersonesos earlier than the fourth century BCE. Ege Yayinlari, The Gravestones of Chersonesos, 2006, p. 14. Gravestones tell of pursuits of those memorialized. Soldiers were depicted with a sword in their belt; vintners by a vine pruning tool, at 54.

When Greeks gained access to the Black Sea, they first settled along the southern shore near ancient Sinope and Trebizond. They fished and smoked fish for transport to Greece. The Black Sea was rich in freshwater fish, swimming counterclockwise across southern shores.

Greek Theatre in Chersonesos

Once established on the Black Sea, Greeks quickly realized the value of being a seaport to receive trade from ancient caravan routes from Persia, headed across the land to the mouth of the Danube and onward to access trade in the Baltic. Greek sailors offered expedient travel by sea and additional markets in Greece.

Over time, southern Black Sea Greeks became curious about the north shore. The estuary of the Dniester River at ancient Olbia, now Odessa, was another source of trade coming from the north of Russia and as far away as the Baltic. There was new wealth to be made from expanded trade and an appreciative Athens to receive it.

Greeks were expert sailors, so sailing north to the Crimean Peninsula presented little difficulty. How the site of the future city of Chersonesos was chosen is unknown. It sits between a quiet bay, from which there is a view of the Sea. The main structures of city life, the theatre, an agora, or main plaza, were built around the bay. Temples and homes were built above the beach. Walking down to the beach today, from the high point at the plaza, now the site of the Orthodox Church, provides a stunning view of the sea and light breezes. The residential area of Chersonesos was an ideal homesite for people of any time in history.

The site of Chersonesos was located in a region where Greeks competed for residence with prior resident barbarian Scythian tribes. The young city was protected by city walls. Farms were ineffectively fortified. The most successful means of protecting crops and trade was in making alliances with Scythian tribes, who found it profitable to work with the new Greeks.

Scythians who turned from fighting Greeks to growing grain for export to Greece found themselves wealthy. They also enjoyed importing Greek wine. Chersonesites coined the term *Scythian boozing*, to reflect upon immoderation of Scythians who imbibed freely.[48]

---

[48]   Paul Hermann, Conquest by Man, Harper & Brothers, New York, 1954, p. 100.

By the fourth century BCE, almost a million bushels of wheat and corn annually left Chersonesos for Athens. This amounted to almost fifty percent of grain consumption in Greece. Back in mainland Greece, farmers were more interested in profitable crops grown in less space, such as olives, figs, grapes and violets. Hot-house violets were available in winter for luxury-oriented consumers in Greek cities. As the needs of Greece for basic food supply grew, Chersonesos received grain from the north in Russia, to as far away as Kiev. The prosperous seaport of Chersonesos, on the Black Sea, held a monopoly on feeding grain to Greece.

So far from Greece, and little known to Athenian society, but for the grain arriving in the port, Chersonesos was not subject to societal hierarchy in long-established society in Athens. Adventurers and farmers coming to the Black Sea were independent entrepreneurs, with opportunities for wealth unknown to them back home. Rank and social position did not transfer from Athens to the Black Sea. All men were equals.

In the growing settlement of Chersonesos, farmers made joint decisions for the good of all. There was no local government to control them, so they controlled the government. Athenian notions of democracy flourished in Chersonesos, as it contributed to a successful farm and export economy.

Archaeologists who study Chersonesos in great detail, have found typical Greek slave names among free citizens of responsibility and affluence in the city.[49] It is possible that Greek former slaves came to Chersonesos, or the names were given to local inhabitants, who quickly merged into Chersonesos society. Either way, the names represent the core value of Chersonesos, and that was democracy. Establishment of a successful settlement, far from home, on new and hostile turf, required solidarity of purpose and heightened the importance of the individual within the group.

---

[49] Richard Posamentiv, Chersonesos Studies I, University of Texas Press, Austin, 2011. Burials at Chersonesos are unique in that family vaults were created in an in-ground cylinder and the remains of deceased were placed into receptacles embedded onto the walls, keeping the center opening circular. Burial containers formed rows of receptacles, some two-dozen deep down the wall, each chamber dedicated to one or more families, at 387.

The most important document in Chersonesos, and one of the most important ancient documents known in the history of the Black Sea region, is the Tablet of the Oath of Chersonesos. It was created sometime between the late fourth century and the early third century BCE, during the height of commercial activity. On the stone tablet was chiseled the oath to be taken by each citizen every year. The Tablet stood in the agora, the main meeting and shopping area of Chersonesos, the area now occupied by the cathedral. Taking the oath was a condition of citizenship. It was the hallmark of Chersonesos democracy.

In brief, the oath of Chersonesos required each person to swear by Zeus, and other Greek gods, to act for the protection and in the interests of people of Chersonesos. Democracy was the obligation of every citizen to protect, foster, and to take no action in derogation of the form of Chersonesos government. Grain could be sold only to benefit Chersonesos.

Control by Emperors and Kings

As the settlement of Chersonesos grew, an administrative organization was necessary. Committees were formed. One group was responsible for building walls and another for demarcation of vineyards. The strategic group was responsible for military decisions and the large and most powerful group determined rules of trade. There were rules for civil order, enforced by another group. As the city became larger and more successful, wealthy merchants participated on several committees. Even in a democracy, wealth fostered power.

The success of Chersonesos is seen in its growth. As additional land was cultivated, more guard towers were built to warn of attack from wandering tribes of prior local residents. Although Chersonesos had no standing army, a temporary and volunteer force convened when there were battles with Scythian bands.[50] Greeks expanded territory by hostile taking of turf when necessary.

---

[50] Scythians were nomadic bands from the area of Iran. From the fourth century BCE to second century CE, competition with more powerful kingdoms around the Black Sea led to demise of Scythia.

Scythians, who grew wealthy from trade relations with Chersonesos, built settlements not far from the Greek city. They grew in force to threaten the Greeks. Chersonesos reached out to nearby friendly kings for protection. Military protection came at a cost.

The growing military power of the Black Sea region was the Pontic kingdom, which grew around the Pontic River in Turkey. In the second century BCE, Chersonesos entered into a treaty with Pontic King Mithradates. Mithradates was an accomplished military leader and the most ruthless of kings in an era of marauding armies. His generals engaged the Scythians several times on behalf of Chersonesos, protecting their city and crops.[51] In payment, Mithradates took control of the entire city and its commercial benefits. Chersonesos was safe and declining in vibrancy.

In 63 BCE, Mithradates died and Romans took the spoils of battle, which included Chersonesos. Julius Caesar had other priorities and granted independence to Chersonesos in 45 BCE. Savvy to realities of protecting their domain, the city fathers of Chersonesos kept an active relationship with Rome, the powerful empire of the century.[52]

The first two centuries of the Christian era brought Roman soldiers to Chersonesos. Rome's purpose was not to threaten democratic, successful, and lucrative Chersonesos, so much as its strategic position on the Black Sea provided an attractive post from which to mount campaigns to further its empire. The power of Rome was descending. Still, it provided Chersonesos centuries more of peaceful trade from the economic center of the Black Sea and enabled cultural development to continue. Rome left local matters to the citizens of Chersonesos and they reciprocated by handing all foreign and military matters to Rome.

During the pendency of the Roman protectorate of the Greek city, temples were built and smaller houses were replaced with larger residences. Chersonesos

---

[51] See generally, Laurent Chrzanouski and Denis Zhuravley, Lamps from Chersonesos, in the State Historical Museum, Moscow, L'ERMA di Bret Schneider publisher, Rome, 1998.

[52] Chersonesos official website: www.chersonesos.org. World Heritage Site designation was awarded in 2013.

was never so grand as Rome or Athens, after all, it was a trade center of the distant provinces. By Black Sea standards, Chersonesos was a stand-out city. The theatre had an elaborate stage, and the funerary monuments displayed a high quality of workmanship.

Chersonesites dined on plates with painted and glazed designs; the artwork of which was simple, countrified and plentiful. Trade-ware included glass from the range of Mediterranean and Baltic ports. At the time of Christ, Chersonesos had access to the best goods of the known world. Two thousand years later, remains of dwellings and trash heaps were records on life to archaeologists.

Chersonesos Museum

The Christian Millennium

The evolution of the Roman world from pagan to Christian is easily seen in Chersonesos, even though the population remained overwhelmingly Greek over the centuries. The first Christian Roman emperor Constantine established Constantinople as his capital. In the breakup of the Roman empire into four parts, under Constantine's predecessor, Diocletian, Constantine took over the eastern sector, that of Byzantium. Eastern Orthodox Christian became the religion of the Byzantine Empire, of which Chersonesos was a distant part. Altars in pagan temples became altars of Christian priests, where carefully and artfully copied books of scripture rested.[53]

Chersonesos took center stage in early developments of Christianity and the development of Eastern Orthodoxy. At the end of the first century CE, St. Clement was exiled from Rome to Chersonesos, where he died at the hands of Greek pagans in the city. The act of the Roman emperor in his choice of venue for banishment shows faith in the city as an armed bastion of Roman troops, at a safe distance from Rome, on the fringe of the empire. Death of the saint caused no insurrection of Christians in Rome.

In the fourth century CE, Emperor Constantine is credited with making a stop in Chersonesos to collect relics of Saint Clement, that is, his bones, and transporting them to Rome. In a pledge of faith, clerics in Chersonesos were allowed to keep a few St. Clements relics. Some of these relics were retrieved by later traveling Saints Cyril and Methodius. Remaining church treasures were lost to conquers in the tenth century.[54]

Chersonesos historians peg Christianization of the city to the sixth century. At about the same time, the name of the city was known as *Cherson*, the Christian city. Growth of the power of the church added a new dimension to Chersonesos democracy. The Byzantine church was ruled from Constantinople, had local bishops in major cities, and dictated certain lifeways. Citizens of Chersonesos were no longer pagan, although they were long civilized. They became accustomed to sharing decision-making with the head of the church. For them, sharing authority with the church was preferable to being subjugated to monarchs of a foreign power.

Powerful and popular Russian military leader Vladimir of Kiev was baptized in Chersonesos in 988, giving the city prominence as the leading church of Russian Orthodoxy.[55] In the nineteenth century, when veneration of all sites

---

[53] Pagan temples had no seating gallery and neither do Eastern Orthodox Churches.

[54] The Basilica of St. Clement in Rome is one of the oldest churches. It sits just beyond the Coliseum, where it holds crypts of Saints Clement, Cyril and Methodius.

[55] The National Preserve of Tauric Chersonesos, 2010.

associated with Vladimir was popular, finding the church of Vladimir led to funding for scientific investigation at Chersonesos. The present church in the ancient city is named for him.

Two factors leading to the downfall and burial of the thriving port of Chersonesos were competition and invasion. In the thirteenth and fourteenth centuries, rising powers of commerce at sea were Genoa and Venice. In the medieval world of commerce, it was not necessary to support great numbers of troops to control land. The competing cities of the east and west coasts of modern Italy cared only to control ships. Launching superior numbers of rowed galleys, eventually replaced by ships of sail, meant controlling the means of commerce. Fields of grain were still harvested in Chersonesos and brought to port; however, the merchants who controlled prices and profits were Italian. Chersonesos lost its monopoly in feeding Athens.

The new powerful armies on land were those of the Tartars, whose skills on horseback brought them from the highlands of Asia west to the Black Sea. While Ottoman Turks sought to conquer lands of present-day Turkey and move west to Greece, with designs on Hungary as a door to Europe, Tartars

Looking across the bay from ancient Chersonesos to modern Sevastopol

moved across the north shores of the Black Sea and Crimean Peninsula. Chersonesos was in the path of Tartars. This time there was no Roman army to stand against invasion.

Toward the end of the thirteenth century, Tartars arrived and ravaged Chersonesos. The massive Tartar army found Chersonesos most attractive as a place to feed their forces. They returned several times for opportunistic grazing, each time leaving the city less able to rebound.

The death blow to Chersonesos came in 1399, when Tartars sacked the city and left it in rubble. Turks came by later and scavenged materials for building in southern Black Sea cities. Chersonesos was left as a pile of stones, its remnant population departing for safer fields.

Four hundred years later, the city of Sevastopol was founded as a military seaport on the Crimean Peninsula. British troops arrived in 1836 to fight a war, in which they were defeated by weather before shots were fired. The new city development and the war transpired as though ignorant of the great city, which once flourished down the beach and sharing the same bay.

Discovery and Preservation of the Russian Pompeii

Archaeologists took an interest in Chersonesos at the end of the nineteenth century. A museum of artifacts from the city was begun in 1892. The present museum building dates to 1902.

Ruins of Chersonesos were evident to Russian military commanders, when developing Sevastopol as a naval port in the late eighteenth century. The site was mapped to the extent remains were evident from the surface. In building the new city of Sevastopol, the site of Chersonesos was avoided.

Avoidance was not preservation. Residents of Sevastopol spent recreational time digging for artifacts as though buried treasure might be found. The site yielded grave markers and household goods, which are valuable information for scientists, and mere curiosities to collectors. From 1805, Russian officials sought to curb destruction and the antiquities market. As Sevastopol grew in population, monitoring protection of Chersonesos was an impossible task.

Odessa founded a Society for History and Antiquities in 1839. Scope of Society interest was the whole northern Black Sea region. The Crimean War halted investigation of the site, as did occasional plague running through Sevastopol, although grueling winters offered seasonal protection from pilfering. Chersonesos was heralded within Russia as the Cradle of Orthodoxy. Later the site was compared to Pompeii in its possible interest to historians.

In the mid-nineteenth century, in a nod to the history of the church in Chersonesos, Tsar Nicholas I approved a new church and monastery built amid the city site. Fortunately, the Church now sits on the ancient site of the open agora, the market square. Main archaeological sites of city cultural activities are closer to the bay in front of the church and the main living sites are at the back of the church as the slope runs down to the beach. Today, the church is seen at the highpoint of terrain, amid the ancient city site. Occupation of the church and monastery made it possible to monitor activities on the Chersonesos city site and curb looting and destruction.

The Nicholas I era church and monastery were destroyed during the Crimean War. St. Vladimir's Church and monastery have since been rebuilt. They give

Interior Byzantine Orthodox Church in Chersonesos

a modern look to the city, as though it has been continually habituated since early Greeks arrived 2,400 years ago. Visitors to the site today experience only an archaeological site, although they can see over house ruins to appreciate the beauty of the area, which so attracted Greeks, to make it their home so far from Athens.

Church bells in the Chersonesos church have their own story. They were cast in 1850, from Turkish guns captured in 1778. The bells were removed and taken to France by French troops in 1856. In 1913, the original bells were returned to Sevastopol and rehung in the church.[56]

Comparison of Chersonesos to Pompeii in 1887, was the promotion campaign of Countess Praskov'ya Uvarova, the head of the Moscow Archaeological Society. She knew that knowledge of the past is the result of organized,

---

[56] The National Preserve of Tauric Chersonesos, 2010, at 15.

systematic data retrieval. Preserving the site for science became her passion. It is to the Countess that Chersonesos, and by extension Sevastopol, which benefits from tourism, owes its greatest tribute. She pressed Tsar Alexander III to fund science at Chersonesos and support preservation of the site.

The Countess was a practical person. She knew that the sooner the data was extracted, the more information could be retrieved. Items saved from looters stocked the museum, made of interest to the general public. For Countess Uvarova, knowledge of the past was for the good of the country. Present-day visitors to Chersonesos are her beneficiaries.[57] By 1911, thousands of visitors came to Chersonesos each year. Sevastopol became more than a military port. It became a tourism venue.

---

[57] Biographers of Chersonesos give tribute to Kostsyushko-Valyuzhinich for initial archaeological investigation, building the museum, laying the groundwork for visitor access to the site and planting the gardens. His efforts exposed walls of the city that led others to become interested and undertake further academic study.

BICKERING BROTHERS OF THE LIGHT BRIGADE IN THE CRIMEAN WAR

Crimea is that small peninsula in the center of the Russian northern half of the shoreline of the Black Sea. In the deconstruction of the Soviet Union, Crimea was part of Ukraine. In the twenty-first century, the Crimea was joined with Russia. In history, just before the American Civil War, from 1854 to 1856, the Crimea was the scene of major battles of a world war, that no one wanted, that gained nothing and is regarded in British, French and Russian history as the least favorite of international skirmishes. Americans learn little of the Crimean war in school, except vague references to the place where Florence Nightingale earned her fame, or the venue of inspiration for the poem of Lord Alfred Tennyson, *Charge of the Light Brigade.* The Crimea is accessed today on a port stop in Sevastopol, a Russian navy town, layered in history.[58]

Tennyson's poem was penned just weeks after the tragic charge of troops of the British Light Brigade. The order to advance into battle, that caused 675 horsemen to ride senselessly to their peril, was given by one of the two main characters of this story and received by the other. These British officers were brothers-in-law, whose ongoing rivalry and petty arguments prolonged the war, needlessly cost the lives of hundreds of soldiers, and eventually became the call for fundamental change in the British military establishment. This is the story of Lord James Thomas Brudenell, the 7th Earl of Cardigan and his brother-in-law, Lord George Charles Bingham, the 3rd Earl of Lucan, as they reached the zenith of their pettiness in the Crimea.

---

[58] Conventional spelling is used throughout. A Russian "v" is pronounced "b" leading to different phonetic spellings. Historic photos are from the US Library of Congress collection on the Crimea.

Two other major factors in this story are Crimea geography and cholera. The Crimea is not an easy place to visit for the unprepared. It is hot in the summer and very cold in the winter. As the brothers learned, too late and to their demise, horses and men could as easily die in the summer heat as the winter cold, without aiding their demise with battles. Those who the weather or guns did not claim, were often victims of cholera, the disease which was at peak epidemic in mid-nineteenth century Crimea.

The Church-Key Dispute that Ignited a War

Exposed Archaeology in the Church of Nativity in Bethlehem

The futile Crimean War began in a dispute over a church-key. The church was no ordinary parish church. The object of controversy was the Church of the Nativity in Bethlehem, built over the site of the stable in which Christ was born. In the mid-nineteenth century, an argument began between Orthodox Armenian and Roman Catholic monks for control of this holiest of Christian

Contested Chapel in the Church of the Nativity

places.[59] Armenian monks possessed the only key to the front door, so they forced the Catholics to enter through the side door. Catholics were barred from use of a chapel.

Then the unthinkable occurred at the Church of the Nativity. Armenians took down the Latin star that Catholics had placed on the manger scene. Monks were seen fist-fighting in the streets of Bethlehem. Some monks died in the fray. All of Jerusalem was in an uproar.

In 1852, at the time of the monks' cabal, Jerusalem was within the Ottoman Turkish Empire. The Turkish Muslim government had no desire to be thrust within a religious war. Ottomans were ecumenical about their population. *Pay taxes to the empire and pray as you wish,* was their operating philosophy for centuries. To resolve civic unrest, the Turks brought in Islamic Scholars

---

59 Clive Ponting, The Crimean War: The Truth Behind the Myth, Chatto & Wundus, London, 2004.

as neutral parties to draft a peace agreement and ensure equitable access of disparate religious orders to the church. The Christians refused to be calmed.

Sitting safely away in Moscow, Czar Nicholas I saw himself as protector of Orthodox Armenians, as he made plans to invade Turkey, his southern neighbor on the Black Sea. Even further away, in exile in England, Louis Napoleon sought to enlarge his status as the heir apparent to the title of Napoleon III. He used the press to inflame tensions as he sought to obtain the favor of French Catholics. Napoleon's actions raised tension between Catholics in Austria and France, but the Austrian emperor did not take the bait. Austria desired to remain neutral in a war that would involve her large eastern neighbors. Years later, wise Austria was the major force in fashioning a peace accord to end the folly of all, who chose to move to a battle that began in a church.

In 1852, the Ottomans gave the church keys to the Church of the Nativity to the Roman Catholics. On behalf of Russian Orthodoxy, Russia considered the decision justification to go down the western edge of the Black Sea and enter Ottoman territory as far as the Danube River. The French declared their allegiance to Turkey, and Britain declared their allegiance to France. The Crimean war began as monarchs of two long-time enemies and Christian countries, France and Britain, aligned with a Muslim country to fight a Christian monarchy. War preparations began full tilt.

The war might have ended in 1854, right after the first shots were fired, except for vanity of the commanders. The initial goal of the allied armies of France, Britain, and Turkey, was to drive the Russians back across the Danube. In so doing, the Russian navy was to be contained and foiled in any attempt to control access to the Black Sea. The French had ground troops, but the hero of the day was the British navy in a quick victory over the Russian navy. Any strategic purpose to justify battle was quickly achieved.[60]

---

[60] In attacking Russia, Britain forfeited a most favored nation trade status with Russia, begun in 1553, when English captains met Ivan IV (Terrible Ivan) in the White Sea. See Cruise through History, Itinerary XII Port of Archangel.

Earl of Cardigan Style of his 11th Hussars – photo US Library of Congress

By the time the British ground forces landed in Varna in 1854, on the west coast of the Black Sea, the Turks had pushed the Russians north of the Danube without assistance from the allies. The Turkish objective was satisfied. Turkish troops packed up to return to base.

British and French commanders preferred to sail across the Black Sea to Sevastopol, a port of the Crimean Peninsula, where they could engage the

Russian fleet in a more suitable conquest, deserving of accolades back home. Their action added two bloody years to a ground war, where neither fleet played a decisive part. Lacking a strategic military purpose, nothing was achieved.[61]

Sevastopol Harbor During the War – Photo US Library of Congress

Looking Lovely in their Uniforms

Lord Lucan, born in 1800, and Lord Cardigan, born in 1797, were handsome men, emblematic of English aristocrats of their time. Their competition blossomed into such hatred for each other that it became a newsworthy

---

[61] The Church of the Nativity in Bethlehem has entered into a new phase of controversy in the 21st century. The area, a market center since before the birth of Christ, is a market center today. In Bethlehem, a Muslim city, merchants observe prayer five times each day, often in or near their shops. As a place of prayer, a Mosque is now planned on the edge of the Church of the Nativity, of a size to obscure view of the church.

story in their time.[62] Their ultimate act of disdain was the moment in which Lord Lucan gave Lord Cardigan the order that sent the later down the valley of death in the most senseless act of the senseless war. It was not their final argument.

Lord Cardigan had a noble lineage that dated back to when King James I started the Order of Barons in 1611. The Cardigan family name went back to the 1300s. With his blond hair and blue eyes, Cardigan was regarded as beautiful and brave, although not at all intelligent. Cardigan was raised in a home of six lovely sisters, who considered him, as did he, the center of all attention. At age fourteen, he suffered a fall from a horse that left him physically unimpaired but mentally changed. He was regarded as impatient and easily angered. He left school for a grand tour in Russia, Sweden and Italy until an uncle gave him a seat in the House of Commons for Marlborough.

Cardigan met his future bride, Elizabeth Johnstone, in Paris, where he had gone to party, and she went to escape a boring marriage. Elisabeth's husband sued Cardigan for alienating the affections of his wife. The Court awarded Captain Johnstone £1,000.[63] Just before the wedding, Cardigan became a Captain in the royal army, at age 29. Such commissions were bought rather than earned.

Cardigan believed his position in society gave him a divine right to lead, in Parliament, as well as the military. He had nice new uniforms designed for his officers and for their horses. The troops were expected to dine on French food. He drilled his troops relentlessly, as though preparing for a parade was a measure of good leadership. When an officer complained, Cardigan pursued the man for court-martial. The matter resolved when the man was found not guilty and Cardigan was relieved of his command.

Cardigan appealed to the Duke of Wellington to restore him to command. The Duke was aware of the younger Lord's reputation and of the 1832 Reform Act in Parliament that weakened Tory aristocratic control. Cardigan persisted along family lines. His sister Harriet married a Lord who was a favorite of Queen Adelaide, Queen to William IV. The press complained of intrigue, but

---

[62] Cecil Woodham-Smith, The Reason Why, McGraw-Hill, New York, 1954.
[63] About $30,000 in 21st century value.

the royal network paid off, and the House of Commons eventually supported Lord Cardigan. In 1836, his father, the 6th Earl of Cardigan, paid £40,000, and Cardigan became a Lieutenant Colonel and commander of the 11th Light Dragoons.[64] He was not yet 40 years old. He had not yet experienced service in combat.

Not much was learned by Cardigan during his hiatus from command. Once restored, he had an officer arrested for pouring the wrong wine at a dinner party. All of his experienced officers, those with actual battle experience in India, joined in protest of his actions. Cardigan was booed in public. He was censured in 1841, for flogging an officer on Easter Sunday and reprieved by the Duke of Wellington in the name of army discipline. The press had a field day with the story.

Next, Cardigan was party to a dueling incident. Dueling was no longer fashionable in the nineteenth century. It was unlawful. Cardigan was convicted of dueling and of giving his counterpart standard pistols, while he held superior hair-trigger pistols. He was acquitted at trial in Parliament, on a technicality. The Christian name of the victim could not be identified, so there was no identifiable victim. The acquittal came after Cardigan transferred his assets to a nephew, in the event that he was convicted.

Buoyed by his triumph in the face of prosecution for his follies, Cardigan pestered Sir Robert Peel for higher office in Parliament and requested that the Queen admit him to the prestigious Order of the Garter. Neither public figure responded to his requests. Homelife was similarly unrewarding. His wife found the company of others to be more fun and Cardigan responded by fathering a whole village worth of offspring in Northampshire.[65]

---

[64] Payment of £40,000 was equal to a full year's income from the elder Cardigan's stables at the time of payment and is equal to $1 million in present day. Purchase of a commission was standard procedure. The usual rate for Cardigan's commission was £5,000, or about $150,000 today. The exorbitant price was set because the elder Cardigan had the means to pay and the younger Cardigan wanted badly to achieve a rank he had not earned. Alexis Troubetzkoy, A Brief History of The Crimean War, Carroll & Graf Publishers, New York, 2006, p. 24.

[65] Woodham-Smith, p. 89.

Sevastopol Monument to Crimean War

In contrast to the family history of Lord Cardigan, Lord Lucan came from recent noble stock. His grandfather was the first Earl of Lucan. The Lucans were a family of soldiers of fortune, who ended up on the right side at the right time. Land given to the First Earl of Lucan was in Ireland. Lucans were absentee landlords of a conquered land. The Second Earl of Lucan loved to party. He resembled Cardigan in living off of the family name and carrying off a married woman, whose husband sued for the loss.

Unlike Cardigan, the Third Earl of Lucan saw active military service at an early age. He became a professional soldier at age sixteen. Although his commission was also purchased, Lucan attained the rank of Lieutenant Colonel by the time he was twenty-six, in part by valor in active service. Cardigan was still a Captain at twenty-nine. The Duke of Wellington had a genuine regard for Lucan. Lucan was an intelligent and capable officer. He was also regarded as obstinate, easily irritated and full of pride.

Lucan married Cardigan's sister, Anne Brudenell, in 1829. At the time of the wedding, Lucan was recently returned from the Balkans, where he had served the Russian Prince Woronzow in action against the Turks. Lucan received a distinguished service medal for his leadership. Not only was Lucan as good-looking as Cardigan, but he was also younger and a decorated soldier, who outranked Cardigan. Cardigan touted his longer lineage. The two egos could not survive at close range.

Lucan inherited a home in London on the banks of the Thames called Laleham. He also was responsible for family lands in Ireland. Both properties were in disrepair. The overseer of the Ireland estate hired most of his extended family in the village. While they lived off of Lucan finances, the locals produced almost nothing from the land. Lucan opted for the status of half-time in the military, analogous to leave without pay so that he could attend to family finances.

Lucan's first task was to fire the locals. He then improved the property with a dairy and stables. The effort and expense could not have come at a worse time. The potato blight struck Ireland, rendering thousands unemployed and hungry. Townspeople blamed Lucan for their troubles, even as he emptied his coffers to feed them.

While Parliament debated whether Lucan was shirking his responsibility to the poor, his wife repeatedly complained to her brother that her husband was giving her insufficient funds to go shopping in Paris. Then life took a downward turn for Lucan. Cholera struck the starving poor of Ireland. Lucan used his troops to tear down rat-infested public buildings and decrepit shacks, leaving him open to accusations in 1847, of causing the deaths of thousands of homeless poor in the snow. Back in London, the Queen's sacred swans were proliferating at Laleham, leaving a mess as a large contained population of swans will do.

By the time of the Crimean War, Lord Cardigan was fifty-seven, and Lord Lucan was fifty-four. Their protector and personal mediator, the Duke of Wellington, died in 1852, at the start of hostilities. Lucan was still feeling fit, but Cardigan was beginning to slow, suffering from chronic bronchitis. Neither man was in a strong financial or social position. Both men hoped to achieve lasting glory in a foreign war.

Charge of the Light Brigade

The acrimony between Lord Lucan and Lord Cardigan was legendary in their own time. By continual fighting between themselves, they narrowed their own possibilities in politics, the military and in society. The Duke of Wellington became fatigued by their quarrels. Upon his death in 1852, Wellington was succeeded as commander in the field in the Crimea, and in the cross-hairs of complaints of the battling brothers-in-law, by Lord Raglan.

Lord Lucan was chosen for command in Crimea in February 1854, before Britain formally entered the war. On April 1, 1854, Cardigan became brigadier general in command of the Light Brigade under Lord Lucan. The press found the situation quite humorous. It remained to be seen whether Cardigan would accept orders from Lucan.

From his first landing in a Black Sea port, Cardigan took the opportunity to humiliate Lucan. Lucan arrived in Varna and began to drill his cavalry. Horses fell dead in the heat after being crammed into ships for the long transport. Meanwhile, Cardigan dined with Napoleon III and his Countess

Eugenie in England, before touring the sites along the route to Varna, as though he was on a pleasure tour. Cardigan bypassed meeting Lucan in Varna and set up camp in the small, lovely, cholera-free town of Deuna, without a word to Lucan.

When the Turks freed Silesia from the Russians, effectively achieving the objective of the war, Cardigan chased after the Russians to monitor the retreat. He claimed victory in war by his actions, in the name of the British, and was promoted to major-general, over the objection of Lucan. As Cardigan's Light Brigade pranced back and forth along the Danube, without fear of taking fire, Russian troops were, in fact, on a hill above, watching with amusement the British dance. The Russians did not attack. They could see that the allies were poorly provisioned and knew that winter and cholera would save Russia the trouble of engaging the enemy.

The ultimate snub to Lucan came from Lord Raglan. He ordered Lucan to remain in Varna, while Cardigan sailed north in the Black Sea to a harbor west of Sevastopol. This area became the allied theater of war to destroy Russian control of the Black Sea.

Lucan was determined to race Cardigan to Sevastopol. Lucan's few ships left Varna so quickly they were not restocked with food and freshwater. Wives of departing soldiers jumped on the ship at the last moment, determined not to be left behind in a strange and cholera ridden place.

The trip across the Black Sea should have taken three days. The trip took seventeen days, while Lucan and Cardigan jockeyed for priority position in the harbor. Food and water on all the ships became depleted. Sanitary conditions caused many men to succumb to cholera. Horses died on the spot where they were tied to swaying sides of the ships.

Away from misery on the troop transports, Cardigan dined on a sparsely boarded steamer, with his guest, the Lady Duberly. When the allies finally landed, they easily captured the town of Eupatoria, with its ghost population of cholera victims. The townspeople hoped the allies would bring aid. Instead, the conquerors were in as bad a shape as the vanquished.

The first engagement with the enemy came on September 19, 1854. As Lucan's cavalry progressed south and around Sevastopol, at the point of Bulganik, on the way to Balaclava, they became lost in the woods. Lucan was blamed for taking the wrong road. By accident, Cardigan came across a line of the Russian army as it retreated from Sevastopol and away from Lucan. Under light fire, Cardigan took a few prisoners, but did not interrogate them, thus depriving Lucan of the intelligence that Sevastopol was undefended and could have been easily taken at that time.

As Cardigan prepared to charge a band of what he thought was a few hundred Cossacks, Lucan sent word to stand down. Cardigan began to pout, unaware that Lucan had saved his life. Lucan could see from his vantage point what Cardigan could not. Waiting for Cardigan to charge forward were thousands of Russians waiting in the woods. Some historians credit Lord Raglan with giving Lucan the order that saved Cardigan, assuming that Lucan would not have been so benevolent of his own volition.

On October 13, the British were in sight of the harbor near Balaclava. Feeling secure, Lord Cardigan ordered his racing yacht brought into the harbor. While the troops and most of the officers slept each night in wet, cold and muddy conditions, Cardigan dined on his yacht each night after taking a warm bath. Lord Lucan referred to Cardigan as the *featherbed colonel*. Troops held Lucan in equal disdain. They referred to Lord Lucan as *Lord Look-on*, for his repeated failure to engage the enemy.

For the British, the day of infamy in the Crimea came on October 25, 1854. On that day, Russians amassed troops on the north side of a valley, with the intent of cutting off supplies from the harbor to the allies. The allies had their backs to Russian troop maneuvers as they were still concentrating on taking Sevastopol to the south. The British ignored all intelligence given to them by Turkish troops. Reconnaissance was an unknown tool for the British, gentleman's army.

Lord Raglan sent four messages on that fateful day, through Lord Lucan. The morning of battle began early, and Lucan and Cardigan missed the first skirmishes while they overslept. As the Russians massed on highpoints of the valley, Turkish troops ran for the harbor. Only Colin Campbell's Scottish

Into the Valley of Death - photo US Library of Congress

Highlanders, in their red waistcoats, stood in a thin red line between the Russians and the ill-prepared allied guns. Campbell's men bravely withstood the Russian assault, throwing the Russians into disarray. The first order that morning delivered by Lucan, late, was for Campbell to do that which he had already done.

Lucan then ordered Cardigan to respond when engaged by the enemy. Cardigan allowed turmoil in the Russian ranks to go unanswered, while Cardigan quibbled with Lucan over whether being five hundred feet from battle constituted *engagement*. Meanwhile, the Russians regrouped. Any possibility of gaining victory in the day vanished, while the brothers-in-law quibbled over terms.

Next, Raglan sent an order to Cardigan to take guns up to the hills and protect the supply road, with support from the infantry. While Cardigan again waited for the infantry to move into a suitable position, Russians began to capture guns belonging to the British. The supreme insult to any army commander was to have his guns captured. Raglan was irate.

The fourth-order given by Raglan to Lucan that day has been the subject of an extended military investigation, hundreds of treatises, and a famous poem. Raglan ordered Lucan to attack the guns with the Light Brigade and then added orally, *immediate*. The order from Raglan to Lucan was delivered by a young expert horseman named Nolan. Nolan road down the hill from Raglan's vantage point, anxious to deliver the order that would end the stall in British action. The written order was to take the guns. Lucan asked, "which guns?" Nolan is believed to have pointed over his shoulder, pointing in his haste and impatience due north up the valley to the well-protected Russian guns, rather than the closer and less well-protected guns being removed by the enemy. Nolan said, "those guns!"

Lucan went to Cardigan to deliver the message. Cardigan questioned, riding straight into heavy enemy fire. Lucan said, "Raglan will have it." Cardigan then said, "Well, here goes the last of the Brudenell's."[66] Without sounding a charge, Cardigan led his Light Brigade into a walk, then a march and finally a trot, straight into heavy Russian cannon fire.

Cardigan rode straight into the guns as though on his death ride. He rode in such a state of rapture that he did not initially realize that he had ridden straight through the line of guns and well into the enemy line. The Light Brigade that followed Cardigan was still under fire and taking heavy hits. Cardigan was in a position to inflict mortal damage on Russian gunners but restrained himself as a gentleman did not engage commoners in battle. The job of attacking Russian guns from the side was left to the French, who were the heroes of the day along, with Colin Campbell and a few British officers, with lower social standing and higher intelligence and common sense.

---

[66] Woodham-Smith, p. 233.

Lord Raglan - US Library of Congress photo

As Cardigan rode behind the battle, relatively unscathed, rumors spread that he had not led the Light Brigade. Of the 658 to 675 men who had come east with Cardigan six months earlier, 230 men and 475 horses were killed in the twenty minutes of the charge of the Light Brigade.[67] As for Cardigan, he kept riding until he reached his yacht. He took a bath, drank champagne, had a nice French dinner, and went to bed.[68]

The London Times was quick to run the story of the Charge of the Light Brigade. Three weeks later, Tennyson penned the poem, *The Charge of the Light Brigade*. The poem was as much tribute to the dead in battle as a light on the folly of the commanders. Immortal are the words: *Theirs's not to reason why – Theirs's but to do and die.* Into the Valley of Death rode valiant soldiers and foolish Lord Cardigan. Even when victory in battle stared him at close range, he ignored the opportunity.

Modern Exterior of Church of the Nativity Today

---

[67] Actual casualty numbers vary among historians. Some count members of the Heavy Brigade who gave fire cover to Cardigan as among 600 plus riders. Others count fewer dead as wounded did not all die immediately.

[68] Ponting, p. 133. See also, Trevor Royle, Crimea, Palgrave, New York, 2000.

The military convened a tribunal, which put most of the blame on Lucan for misunderstanding Raglan's order. Cardigan was revered as a hero. He claimed sick leave and returned to London in December to garner his accolades, even as his men, in far worse condition, continued to endure hardships of the Crimea. Lucan was disgraced.

Peace without Victory

Just as inhabitants of Moscow burned their city before the entry of Napoleon I, residents of Sevastopol burned their city before Napoleon III could capture it. Finally, in 1856, the neutral Austrians stepped in to broker a peace accord, which the French and Russians eagerly accepted. The provisions for peace included: 1. Russia would surrender the Danube provinces; 2. The Danube would remain a free navigation river; 3. The Black Sea would be a neutral zone, and 4. Russia would no longer claim to be a protectorate for the Eastern Orthodox in Ottoman Turkey. There was no mention of the church in Jerusalem, or a church-key. The total casualties numbered about 500,000, half for each side. There were no winners in the war.

In June 1855, Lord Raglan died in the Crimea of fever, but not before he saw his troops starve to death. One of Raglan's last tasks was to mediate a dispute between Cardigan and Lucan. Each complained the other misunderstood Raglan's orders of October 25.

Lucan sued the Daily News for disparaging stories. He invested heavily in raising beef in England, just at the time frozen beef from Argentina became available for less cost. He died in England in 1888, at age 88. Lucan's best legacy may be his son and successor, Lord George Bingham, the Fourth Earl of Lucan, who allowed the Irish to buy the land they farmed. He gave township land cleared by his father to the town as a central marketplace. His wife organized a tweed industry in Castlebar. Further, the young Earl allowed Catholics to be educated in their faith.

Lord Cardigan enjoyed his short time in the light of fame. As soon as soldiers who served with him returned from the Crimea, his status as a hero was tarnished. He was called a fake hero in the press. In 1863, Cardigan brought

Sevastopol Memorial to Later Wars

Rebuilt Sevatopol

an unsuccessful defamation action before the Queen's Bench. His wife died, and he married the thirty-year-old daughter of a friend. The Queen did not like his Spanish-dancer wife and banished Cardigan from social circles. He was ostracized by family and had few friends. Cardigan died of a stroke on March 28, 1868, while riding a horse.

The most important postscript to this story was the demise of the English military system as it had been organized since feudal times through the Crimean War. While social status is still important to high rank, ability and experience are given greater weight in commissions.

Much of nineteenth-century Sevastopol was burned during the war, that remains as a tribute to man's vanity in the guise of political need. Thankfully, there is no more cholera. Sevastopol was rebuilt as a beautiful port on the Black Sea. Late nineteenth-century buildings on wide boulevards rose after the war, giving the city a graceful look. The city also hosts fairs and markets. Today Sevastopol is home to the Russian navy. Within walking distance of the dock are memorials to several wars, most fought on foreign soil. Close to the harbor, all is peaceful.

YALTA, UKRAINE

(ANCIENT YALTO)

Yalta's Vorontsov Palace

On the north Black Sea coast, in the Crimea Peninsula, is Yalta, the health spa town of Russian tsars, Communist party leaders, and poets. Early history of the city is characteristic of many cities that ring the Black Sea. It was an ancient Greek outpost, from which grain grown in the region was sent to Athens. In the Byzantine era, Yalta was a seaport of trade, bringing grain from the north and caravan goods from the east, south to Constantinople. Conquered by Ottoman Turks in 1475, liberated by Russia in 1783, and fiercely defended in a war with Turkey, late in the eighteenth century, Yalta gave no hint of its later glory, during its mundane years as a strategic seaport.

In the nineteenth century, Yalta was looked upon throughout Russia as a spa town. In 1889, Tsar Alexander III built an escape from Moscow, the Massandra Palace. The last of the Romanovs, Nicholas II, built the Livadia Palace in 1911, a white confection of long arched porticos and a family chapel. Lesser royals, high court officials and wealthy merchants built their summer dachas in Yalta, close to homes of the rich and powerful. More than simple, typical Russian wooden summer homes, known as dachas, the summer residences of Yalta included many palaces.

Premier Joseph Stalin utilized the Massandra Palace as his private retreat, although Vladimir Lenin previously decreed that Yalta was a health spa destination for workers, not royals. In 1945, the final details of accords from World War II were resolved in the Livadia Palace, by the Big Three; United States President Franklin Roosevelt, United Kingdom Prime Minister Sir

Winston Churchill and Stalin for the Soviet Union. Livadia Palace is now famous as the Yalta Peace Palace.

Yalta Peace Palace – Former Romanov Family Retreat

In the nineteenth century, writers came to Yalta for the quiet and relaxed pace, conducive to long novels and elegant short stories. Leo Tolstoy reflected on *War and Peace* and *Anna Karina* in Yalta. Anton Chekhov built his vacation home, the White Dacha, in 1898. From his window in the White Dacha, Chekhov had a view of the pier where the ferry brought vacationers from big cities. His story of *The Lady with the Dog* is set on that pier, where the lady waited, patiently lost in thought. Today the pier is festive, with a Ferris Wheel and a perennially market fair atmosphere.

Of the many notable visitor points of interest in Yalta, the most intriguing is the Yalta Palace of Count Mikhail Vorontsov. Beyond the royal Romanovs, the Vorontsov's were the first family in the official affairs of Russia. Patriarch of the family, Semyon Vorontsov, was an ambassador to England for Catherine the Great. His children served in Catherine's administration and beyond.

Vorontsov Palace Yalta

Prince Mikhail Vorontsov is well known in Russia as a critical player in the first family of Imperial Russia. Since he was a quiet administrator, not a royal, revolutionary, or soldier, he is not well known outside of Russia. Visitors to Odessa see the official residence of Mikhail as the royal administrator of the city. His tomb is in Odessa. His story extends beyond Odessa, and St. Petersburg, where the family home takes up a full block, on one side of Alexander Nevsky Prospect (Boulevard), opposite the grand home of the merchant dynasty in Russia, the Stroganov Palace.[69]

This is the little story of the grand palace of Yalta, that of the Vorontsov Palace. Lesser known than the White Dacha of Chekov, or white Yalta Peace Palace, it is an architectural marvel of imposing grey stone and fanciful Moorish arches. Vorontsov could build his signature home anywhere in Russia. He chose Yalta, the *yalo*, or the safe shore of ancient Greeks.

---

[69] Stroganov is also spelled Stroganoff. The Stroganov dynasty became wealthy as merchants doing business in Siberia in the sixteenth century, during the time of Ivan IV, also known as Ivan the Terrible.

The Family Vorontsov

The Vorontsov family is of the long-titled lineage that can be traced back to mayors of fourteenth-century Moscow. At times, proximity to power ended in the death of a family patriarch, who came to displease a tsar. The family never entirely dropped from power or wealth. The family home on the main artery of St. Petersburg, Nevsky Prospect, was designed by Rastrelli, the Italian architect to tsars of the eighteenth century, particularly Empress Elizabeth,[70] who is responsible for the grand staircase on which millions of visitors enter the Hermitage Museum. The sprawling grand Baroque Vorontsov estate is a monument to a long-standing royal family by connections to royalty, not of royal blood. Count Semyon Vorontsov was the builder of that St. Petersburg home.

Vorontsov dynastic prominence came to its height under the short reign of Russian Tsar Peter III, the successor to Empress Elizabeth. During Peter's six-month reign, Count Mikhail Illarionovich Vorontsov was the family patriarch and the most powerful man in Russia. His niece Elizaveta was mistress or playmate to the tsar.[71] When Peter III was deposed by his wife Empress Catherine, another of Count Vorontsov's nieces, Yekaterina Romanova Vorontsova-Dashkova, became a high-ranking official in the cabinet of Catherine II. Yekaterina was in charge of education and the arts, favorite projects of the empress, who was soon known as Catherine the Great.

Catherine the Great knew it was better to absorb talent into her administration than to be vindictive and purge the government of Peter's close associates. Counselor to her husband and aide in her taking power, just six months into the reign of Peter III, was Count Mikhail Vorontsov. After the coup, Count Vorontsov was interrogated by Empress Catherine's close supporters. He

---

[70]   Empress Elizabeth, a daughter of Peter the Great, reigned from 1741 to 1762. She commissioned Rastrelli to guild Tsarskoe Selo, the palace dedicated to Catherine I, wife of Peter I, her mother. Elizabeth was a fan of covering wood with gold, known as Rocco style of architecture.

[71]   Peter III was more interested in dressing rats in little military outfits and dispatching them, than in women. While he enjoyed the slide from his second-floor bedroom in Oranienbaum Palace, outside of St. Petersburg, to the snowy bank below, his wife, Catherine translated a French encyclopedia into Russian. Peter spoke only German.

performed as a chancellor, although he never again gained the full power over Russian affairs, that he had previously known. He married a first cousin to Catherine the Great, just as his father married a relative of Tsarina Empress Elizabeth. Power was kept in the family. The Count left the government in 1763 and consoled himself by decorating the palace in St. Petersburg.[72]

Yekaterina founded her off-spring dynasty as a Vorontsova-Dashkova. A Vorontsova-Dashkova descendent distinguished himself as a general, in charge of Russian Imperial troops during World War I. He eventually died in retirement in Yalta. She eventually settled in London. Her two brothers, Alexander and Semyon Romanovich Vorontsov, were Russian diplomats to the tsars. The siblings were all fans of England and English styles.

Semyon Vorontsov was an advisor to Catherine the Great and Russian ambassador to England. His son, Mikhail Semyonovich (son of Semyon) Vorontsov, is known as Prince Vorontsov. As grand-nephew to his namesake Mikhail, the Prince was also a general in the Imperial Army of Russia. He was an advisor to Tsar Alexander I, as was his uncle Alexander Vorontsov. The Prince served in the Caucasus region conflicts and built a palace in Odessa, his base of operations.[73]

Vorontsov Palace in Yalta

Mikhail Semyonovich Vorontsov was born in the Vorontsov St. Petersburg estate in 1782.[74] His father Semyon became the count upon the death of his great uncle, making Mikhail prince and heir apparent as patriarch to the Vorontsov family dynasty. As such, he was bound to build a home of his own appropriate to a man of his standing.

---

[72] Eventually, Count Vorontsov overspent on the palace, exhausted his funds and sold the palace to the government. Tsar Paul I gave the fifty-room estate to the Knights of Saint John Hospitaller, of which he was Grand Master, a position purchased for him by his mother, Catherine the Great.

[73] See the tribulations of the Prince in his dealings with itinerant Russian poet, Pushkin, in this itinerary, Odessa.

[74] Mikhail Semyonovich Vorontsov lived to be seventy-four in 1856. He died in Odessa and his tomb is in the Odessa Cathedral.

Vorontsov Palace Music Room

View from Rear Terrace of Vorontsov Palace

Vorontsov led Russian troops in eight major battles in the Napoleonic wars, the Russian-Turkish wars, and the Caucasian War. He was graced with every top award of the Russian military, a virtual diamond-studded chest array of gold stars. He led Russian troops in the initial Russian taking of Varna. A military legend, Vorontsov was also known for promoting the health of his troops and for keeping the plague out of Odessa, where he was governor-general of New Russia, Ukraine.

The incredibly handsome Vorontsov and his lovely wife had no children. While poet Alexander Pushkin was assigned to duties in Odessa, he and Vorontsov's wife had an affair, one of many affairs for the poet. When Vorontsov was finally able to have the poet reassigned, he left town, leaving a pregnant Elizabeth Vorontsov. Prince Vorontsov spent most of his time not in battle in building a palace for his retirement in Yalta. He eventually succumbed to illness from life under battlefield conditions, never having the planned-for retirement as lord in his Yalta castle.

As one of the wealthiest and most distinguished men of his time in Russia, Vorontsov built what became the largest palace on the Crimean coast, among numerous palaces of the wealthy and royal elita of his time. Known as Vorontsov Palace for its owner, or Alupka Palace for the village near the estate, it was built between 1828 and 1848, years of high glory in the career of the Prince. Forty years later, Tsar Alexander III built the Massandra Palace nearby. The Massandra Palace is also a grand palace, yet not as memorable, nor as large as the Alupka Palace.

Vorontsov chose an English architect for his palace in Crimea, understandable given the affinity of his parents, aunts and uncles for England. The architect, Edward Blore, produced what he envisioned as an Englishman's estate in the Crimea. The result is considered English Renaissance style, which is an eclectic blend of towers and squat eastern domes. Unlike English country homes of the mid-nineteenth century, the Vorontsov Palace has a tall, elongated façade, made interesting by vertical sections. Built of grey, local-quarried stone, it is an imposing palace. Compared to the French Country house blended with Russian dacha style that is the Massandra Palace of Tsar Alexander III, built forty years later, the two palaces are from different worlds.

Facing the front entry to the palace, sharing entry court, to the right, is the entrance to what appears to be a medieval castle. The grey stone façade of the castle is harsh and is used in building round turrets with symmetrical square entry towers and a round guard tower. This fanciful castle entry is the entrance to a mock medieval street, along which is housed servants' quarters and service buildings. The effect of the medieval castle, giving way on the entry court to the English manor house façade, is to suggest the estate is a long-established residence of a dynastic family of means and power.

The interior of the Vorontsov Palace has liberal use of wood paneling and woodblock floors in the one-hundred and fifty rooms. Upper floor bedrooms face the ocean for the view and breezes. Unlike typical English manor houses, or Russian estates, both with a male wing and a female wing, demarked by type of use and furniture style, the Vorontsov Palace is devoid of strict delineation. The lady of the house had a boudoir, which extended into the area usually reserved for a billiard room. Two principle rooms, the dining room and library, were late additions to the palace in a separate wing. The Prince was an admirer of Sir Walter Scott and wished to recreate Scott's library in Yalta.

The Vorontsov Palace was built at the cost of nine million silver rubles. Today, the eighty-four ounces of silver in the rubles would be worth about $1.5 million. In 1848, the amount spent on the palace was staggering. Values are difficult to ascertain and relate to current values. Still, it is safe to say that the commission given Blore was one of the largest private commissions of its day.

Blore was attuned to placing his creations in landscaped luxury. A German landscape designer, Carolus Keebach, was commissioned to create a total environment in ninety-nine acres. Today the house and gardens encompass the Massandra estate. From windows, balconies, and glass-encased halls of a winter garden, views of the surrounding forest give an aura of exclusivity, while the planting beds and rose gardens soften the look of grey stone and provide outdoor spaces for intimate moments in nature.

The Vorontsov Palace has many more windows than the typical Russian estate home. Dachas, lighter, usually wooden summer residences, are built to provide views to a garden. The Palace combines an impressive estate home of a man of consequence, with light and garden views.

Vorontsov Palace Interiors

Other Russian noblemen of the time built two-story, boxy palaces, fronted with columns in a neo-classical style, with long, sometimes curved wings, running from each side of the center square of main entrance and entertaining areas. The exterior of the typical Russian estate home was painted stucco, usually red, as dark red was expensive. The unpainted stone of the Vorontsov Palace, two stories across the full façade, with rows of windows and no columns, was a contrast to its contemporaries. Prince Vorontsov was an elegant, distinguished, and accomplished man who stood above his contemporaries. Well-traveled, he was inspired by new designs. The Vorontsov Palace is a fitting signature of the man.

The Vorontsov Palace of Yalta was not the first palace built by the Prince. In Odessa, he commissioned a palace, which fits in the general genre of estate homes of the Russian gentry. That palace is a boxy, two-story, painted stucco style with Greek columns across the front entry. Lacking are the wings, given the small patch of real estate at the end of the main pedestrian boulevard

Moorish Arch Rear Entry to Vorontsov Palace

that runs along the waterfront. Architect of the Odessa palace was Francesco Boffo, an Italian responsible for thirty buildings in Odessa, by the time of his death in 1861.

There are two distinct faces and moods to the Vorontsov Palace. From the front entry court, the mood is strong, imposing and serious. From the rear, the light, flat-roofed covered patios and balconies are edged by open-work balustrades rather than the heavy stone pillared railing consistent with the stone front façade. The back of the house is ready for an outdoor party. The front faces a stone entry court and the back faces gardens, a quiet inlet of the sea, and forest beyond.

The signature feature at the rear of the palace is the Moorish Arch that opens the rear rooms to the gardens. The entrance to the palace is deep within the arch. The arch is entered from the garden path, not from a carriage drive court, as guests would arrive in the frontcourt. The eastern Moorish appearance of the rear is in stark contrast to the English castle front approach.

Inspiration for the arch is generally attributed to Blore's vision of the mosque in Delhi. The decision to include such an arch began with Vorontsov's prior architect, Englishman Thomas Harrison. Harrison was a classically trained architect; whose liberal use of columns was popular in eighteenth-century England. An early drawing by Harrison places the arch in the exact center of the rear of a boxy two-story main house, with classical wings extending from each side. The design was simply a variation on the standard, with accommodation of the client's requested inclusion of a Moorish arch. Blore integrated the arch into a pleasing, softer design feature.

By the time he commissioned the Yalta project, Vorontsov was well-traveled through England and appreciative of variations in style. After the death of Harrison, rather than employ Harrison's collaborator Boffo, Vorontsov elected for a new approach to his palace. It is also likely that Vorontsov was impressed by the Muslim Tartars, from whom he purchased the property, and who had requested that he build a mosque for their use. If true, the mosque-style arch is a nod to historical residents of the area. Regardless of the reason for the distinctive, prominent feature, the Vorontsov Palace presents a revolution in style that abandons classical columns for a fanciful arch. Vorontsov had prominence in social standing. He could afford to be a maverick.

Visiting Yalta Today

Prince Vorontsov ascended to Count while he completed his palace. His increasing blindness lessened any joy he might have known from occupancy of the Palace. Count Mikhail Vorontsov spent his final years in Odessa, where he died in 1856, and was entombed. Odessa was a distance from the Crimean War raging in the Yalta peninsula, during his final years. That war tore apart his affection for his native country from his adored England. Countess Vorontsov also preferred to remain in Odessa. For her, the draw to life in Odessa was social. Alupka was a country estate.

Heir to the estate of the Count, his only son Prince Semyon Vorontsov[75] married in the Vorontsov Palace. Upon the death of the Prince in 1882, his widow held an estate sale of the palace contents and moved to Paris. Next in line was the Count's daughter, who became Countess Sofia Shuvalova. Sofia spent most of her life estranged from her husband and found the Vorontsov Palace a perfect summer retreat for herself and her three children: Pavel, Mikhail, and Elizaveta.

As the oldest male, Pavel inherited the Palace, which upon his death, went to his brother Mikhail. Neither Pavel nor Mikhail had children, so the last heir standing was their sister Elizaveta. She married a distant cousin, Illarion Vorontsov-Dashkova, bringing the Vorontsov line full circle. Elizaveta made every effort to restore the palace and to repurchase furnishings sold by her aunt. Count Illarion died in the Vorontsov Palace in 1916. In 1919 the Countess sailed for Malta as the Bolshevik Red Russians displaced royals and ministers of Imperial Russia.

In 1921, the nationalized Vorontsov Palace was opened as a state museum. On display in the museum are former possessions of Russians, who attained noble titles from wealth, including Stroganov and Yusupov, in addition to Vorontsov. During World War II, Hitler made the Palace a gift to one of his field marshals, who used it as his headquarters. The final guest of the palace would have pleased its first owner. In February 1945, when the Yalta Conference was held in the Livadia Palace nearby, Sir Winston Churchill was housed in the Vorontsov, Alupka Palace.

---

[75] Prince Semyon Vorontsov was born in 1823 and died in 1882.

Dock Area in Yalta Today – Inspiration for Chekhov's story Lady with a Dog

Today the Vorontsov Palace and Massandra Palace are often joined as shore excursions in Yalta, with a tour of the gardens and grounds. It is not possible to walk the ninety-nine acres of park and forest of the Vorontsov Palace in a single shore visit. A lovely view across the inlet, from the parapet of the Palace garden, suffices to give an idea of the grandeur of the estate. The smaller Massandra Palace sits behind a pond in landscaped gardens, often enjoyed by locals. Both estates have been utilized as movie sets in Russian cinema.

Yalta Peace Palace, the former summer residence of Tsar Nicholas II, intrigues westerners for its connection to the Yalta Conference at the close of World War II. Photos on the walls, showing the Big Three sitting together in the arched porticos of the palace, belie their political tensions. The white palace today is as much a museum piece to the beginning of the Cold War, as it is the final days of the bucolic life of the Romanovs. As history of the first half of the twentieth century dims from recollections of visitors, the palace is a stroll through lovely halls and maintained gardens.

Romanov Family Chapel at Yalta Peace Palace

Interior Corridors of Yalta Peace Palace

When visiting the Vorontsov Palace, remember the man who commissioned the unique manor estate. If the encounter with the arch at the rear is a surprise, think of it as a gift from your benefactor, the man who tangled with Napoleon's forces and impudent poet Pushkin, then left a legacy for visitors to enjoy. It is a pity that he had only a few summers to spend at the palace. Visitors with only a few hours will find time in Vorontsov Palace a memorable experience.

SOCHI, RUSSIA

(ANCIENT DIOSURIUS)

Learning to Love Stalin — Or at Least Stalinist Architecture

Few people today would think of Stalin as a love interest. He is the former Bolshevik brute who pushed aside memories of Lenin's view of Marxist Socialism in a worker's Russia, for a forceful military-based socialist nation. He is most associated with the Siberian Gulag, in which more Russians died than enemies of Russia in war. Nor would many people consider Stalin, an aesthete. Those with good memories of Russian history will recall Stalin's feud with socialist intellectual Leon Trotsky, who championed Lenin style socialism for an international worker's revolution.

Still, Stalin had his moments. Underneath the harsh exterior, there was a soft place in his life for architecture. Stalin was a champion of the socialist realism school of architecture.[76] Not to be confused with social realism or Brutalism. From 1931 until his death in 1953, and possibly onward to 1955, when Nikita Khrushchev called a halt to the excesses of bourgeois extravagance, Stalin and his supporters fostered an ambitious building program in Soviet Russia. It was propaganda in the form of embodiment of the Soviet spirit in iconic, inspirational architecture.

Stalin sponsored international architectural competitions that attracted respected architects, particularly those of the international, minimalist style.

---

[76] Stalin also enjoyed swimming. His residence had a deep pool, although not one conducive to long lap swims.

Many of the commissions awarded as a result of competitions, were executed in Moscow. A collection of these public buildings is also found in Sochi, at the southern tip of Russia, on the Black Sea coast.

A new century building boom in public works was spurred by the 2004 Olympic Winter Games, held in Sochi. The new Sochi airport is an architectural gem, worthy of any major city in the western world. Amidst new structures of steel and glass, the visitor to Sochi will see a sizable number of pre-midcentury, oddly neoclassical, bold, and imposing buildings. Eighty years post erection, the collection of structures becomes a historical study of a cultural era when Soviet Socialists wanted to give the appearance of capitalism, only better. Stalin promoted architecture as ideology. Whether he succeeded is a decision in the view of the visitor to Sochi today.

The Stalinist Socialist Realism architecture to be found in Sochi is the ingénue of this story. If the passage of time may allow past events to be overtaken by the esthetics of the present, the world may come to love, if not Stalin, then Stalinist architecture. The Olympics concluded; the architecture remains, luring curious visitors to the warm, southern city of Russia on the Black Sea.

Sochi Theatre

Getting to Know Stalin

Joseph Stalin was born Iosif Vissarionovich Dzhugashvili in Gori, Russia, in 1878. His father was a cobbler and church-going member of the Georgian Orthodox church. Nothing in his childhood suggests Stalin's later avocations and governing style. Stalin endured a bout of smallpox when he was seven. At twelve, his left arm was permanently damaged in a carriage accident. The disfigurement was sufficient to later provide a release from conscription to fight in World War I. Stalin received a scholarship to a Georgian Orthodox seminary school at sixteen. He did not stay around long enough to take his final exams. By age twenty-five, he was an avowed Marxist and a member of Lenin's Bolsheviks.

Stalin came to well know the Caucasus region at the southern tip of Russia. It was there that he performed as a Bolshevik operative. Stalin raised money for the cause through bank robbery, extortion, and kidnappings for ransom.

Stalin was captured by Royal Tsarist police seven times. Each time he was arrested, Stalin was sent to Siberia. Each time he was incarcerated, Stalin managed to escape. Eventually, he reinvented himself as *Stalin*, the Russian word for steel. This moniker well suited the revolutionary playing an all stakes game of power, for whom prison was no deterrent.

In the Russian civil war of 1917, Lenin gave Stalin and Trotsky equal power. It may have been brilliant of Lenin to include divergent views within the Politburo, but Stalin was much too impatient to allow the intellectual, philosophical views of communism espoused by Trotsky to meld slowly and organically into the fabric of society. Stalin preferred to take the leadership role, take control of the military, and eventually, in 1922, when Lenin suffered a stroke, take political leadership of the country. While he was alive, Lenin sided with Trotsky in disputes between his two deputies. When Lenin died, Trotsky was exiled by Stalin, and Stalin became dictator for life.

Stalin was not a patient man. There is no question that he brought his nation into the twentieth century in a short period. He did so by brute force. Moving an agrarian society into an industrialized nation in short order meant having zero tolerance for dissent. In Stalin's socialism, workers performed as assigned, or were sent to labor camps, exile, or worse. There were initially no social programs in Stalin's socialism.[77]

Sochi Apartment Building for the Elite of thee Politburo

In Stalin's Soviet state, former farmers built roads, over which there were no harvests to take to market. As people starved, they were considered enemies of the state and purged. Morale was as low as a thermometer in a Moscow winter.

---

[77] In the eventual U.S.S.R. there were some groundbreaking social programs for Russia. Girls were entitled to an equal education and had equal rights. The largely illiterate country became largely literate in a generation. There was universal access to healthcare, which may not have been great, but it gave Russians their first generation without typhus, cholera and malaria. Women were given prenatal care. Engineers were coveted, whether educated from within, or imported. Those who performed above quota were able to become — capitalists.

The Second World War was a boon to Stalin. Initially, standing on the sidelines, allowing history to repeat itself, he waited for German aggression to give him the impetus to act. The Germans, like Napoleon more than a century earlier, tried to take Russia in the winter, when the lack of roads and a navigable infrastructure made travel impossible. Under Stalin's command, Russia gobbled up neighbors, captured Berlin, and gained a seat at the table with the superpowers.[78]

Though Stalin's methods for success were more often despicable than not, he moved successfully from gang leader, to military leader, to domestic leader. As ruler of a captive population, it was his choice of which monuments to build, how and where to build them, and what to commemorate. He was wise enough to know that men are mortal, and buildings can be monuments to mortals for eternity. Stalin decided to build monuments to himself in newly styled public works of the new Soviet Russia. He invented a new style for his Union of Soviet Socialists: Socialist Realism. Then he reached out to architects to give form to his idea and built his dream city in Sochi.

Stalin's International Architecture Competition

In 1931, a plan emerged to build defining edifices of the new Soviet nation. The buildings were further propaganda of the glorious supremacy of the ruling party. The Supreme Soviet required a home that gave optics to the power of the men within it. In Stalin's dream city, the *Palace of the Soviets* required a magnificent building evocative of respect and power. This idolatry of communism was more Stalinism than Marxism. The buildings were not places where workers would feel comfortable. Just as churches reach upward as a vision of spirit, Stalin's buildings required a strong stance and a tower of majesty.

Initially, the concept of building public works came out of necessity. In the early twentieth century, Russia was a country with minimal infrastructure. The capital at Moscow was still a dark enclosed fortress within a medieval,

---

[78] Stalin was nominated for the Nobel Peace Prize in 1948.

randomly built city, unlike the beautifully planned city of Peter I of Saint Petersburg renamed Leningrad. The capital city lacked functional canals, streets, and transport mechanisms for the citizenry. Moscow desperately needed a master plan.

After World War II, cities, such as Kiev, renamed Stalingrad, needed rebuilding out of post-war necessity. In the idyllic pre-war period of Stalin's growing power, the challenge was to build his country in his image. The cost of labor and materials was immaterial. Function and quality were not as important appearances, which was everything. Stalin proclaimed a plan and the party gave approval.

In addition to the Palace, party leaders authorized the construction of a Moscow Canal and a Moscow Metro. Designs were solicited from known Russian architects. The 1931 competition resulted in no winners. Either Soviet Russia lacked architects, after years of purges and imprisonment of intellectuals, or none shared Stalin's vision. The competition was reopened later in 1931, on an international scale. Trotsky was unable to bring communism to the west, but the west was invited to send architects to Moscow.

Stalin's timing was good. The western world was at the beginning of the Great Depression. As a result, architectural commissions in the United States and Europe were scarce. Architects are artists, not politicians. The opportunity to design a new Russia was compelling. The call for proposals brought in over one hundred and fifty designs submitted from Soviet and foreign architects. Leading architects such as Ernst May, Albert Kahn, Walter Gropius and Le Corbusier entered the competition. Their modern minimalism, on a grand, Brutalist scale, was consistent with Stalin's self-image of Soviet Realism. Their designs inspired Stalinist buildings. Moscow gained a metro of which it is still proud. Less visual, although necessary, infrastructure projects were begun.

There were two more rounds in the competition between 1932 and 1933. This time entry was by invitation. Stalin chose the winner for the commission to build the Palace of the Soviets. The winners were soviets and partners Boris Iofan and Vladimir Shuchuko. Stalin accompanied the commission with his proposed alterations in the design. If the architects winced, they complied.

Classic Stalinist Architecture at the Port of Sochi

Ultimately the Palace of the Soviets was never built. The one hundred-story tower, with columns at the base and diminishing floor space as it raised wedding cake style to the heavens, was topped with a statue. Stalin's vision was more folly than realistic. He would have been well-served with a stage set, photographed and projected on posters. Few of Russia's agrarian population traveled to Moscow. In the pre-television age, reality was a far-away concept.

The chosen building site was near the Kremlin on the former site of the Cathedral of Christ the Savior. The church was demolished along with religious practice in favor of more politically proper use. Had the palace been completed, it would have been the tallest structure in the world at the time. Construction began in 1937. It was halted upon the 1941 German invasion.

Materials at the building site of the Palace were conscripted for military needs. The steel frame was recycled. Building the Palace did not resume after the war. The site became an open-air swimming pool in 1958. Times changed. Priorities

Stalin's Fortress Retreat in Sochi

Stalin's Vision of Socialist Style Seen in Sochi

changed. In 1995, after the demise of the Soviet Union, the Cathedral was rebuilt at the site, a symbol of the new Russia.[79]

The interest of Stalin in architecture continued after the war. The 1949 Stalin Prize for architecture represented a shift in projects desired for commissions. The three winning post-war project designs were all for apartment projects in Moscow.

One building best represents the architectural politics of the time, the Zemlyanoy Val. Units were designed to be residences for the soviet inner circle. The building is luxurious inside and out. It was praised by Stalin in 1949 and was criticized by his successors in 1953. For Nikita Khrushchev, the building became the poster child for excesses of his predecessors.

---

[79] Russian Orthodox practice is popular throughout Russia today. In spite of almost eighty years of hiatus of religious practice, traditions persevered. Restored churches hold museums of icons and active congregations.

Stalinist architecture can still be seen throughout the former Soviet Union. There are large projects in Poland, Bulgaria, Romania, and East Germany. Soviet embassies, such as the one built in 1952 in Helsinki, are Stalinist classics. The building looks higher than its two floors, with a strident façade of neo-classical columns.[80] By 1955, cost-cutting was in style, and the Stalinist architecture era came to an end.

Stalinist Era Spa for the Proletariat Outside of Sochi

Buildings for the Proletariat

Not all buildings begun during the lifetime of Stalin can be included in the category of Stalinist architecture. Massive, standardized, inexpensively built housing blocks, often equated with post-war Russia, were not within

---

[80]   The Soviet-built embassy in Helsinki, a city of great architecture, looks like an imposing version of the US White House. By comparison, the US Embassy in Helsinki is a bland, two story, non-descript structure, easily mistaken for an apartment house, where function and cost, not design or public statement of image, were priorities.

Stalin's vision of the prestige of Soviet Russia. Those drab structures were the result of later efforts to economize in post-war baby boom cities. The now-classic Soviet apartment blocks provided desperately needed mass housing, rather than existing as definitive public works. The eyesores that are endlessly long apartment blocks, snaking along the horizon, can be attributed to Stalin's successor, Nikita Khrushchev. Disparagingly dubbed *Khrushchyovka*, those buildings resulted when Khrushchev closed the Soviet Academy of Architecture.

Stalinist architecture is an odd blend of traditional construction with bold facades, known as *Constructivism*. In Constructivism architecture, classical pillars are combined with unadorned, massive block, heavy-appearing buildings. There was no one guiding architect to consider a visionary of style. Stalinist architecture is what Stalin envisioned at any given time.[81]

The Stalinist architecture was much like Stalinist politics, heavy-handed expressions of a new order imposed on existing technology. Underneath the massive, wet-stucco walls is simple brick masonry. The roof beams are wood, and the roofs are sheets of metal. None of the elegance of typical church construction is evident. Public edifices of the Stalin era are more like factory buildings, using farm building technology, with imposing facades.

---

[81] Some of Stalin's personal memos on architecture have come to light since 2001, informing scholarly review.

Streetscape Sochi

Devoid of decoration, unique artistic expression, or planning for utility, it would seem that the buildings were quickly and inexpensively constructed. That was not the case. Erecting Stalinist buildings was inordinately expensive, even assuming the availability of cheap labor and materials. The projects were noted for inefficiency. They required substantial manual labor. Every aspect of Stalinist architecture defined Soviet Russia of the 1930s. Large numbers of unskilled labor needed jobs. They came to Moscow, Minsk, Kiev, or Sochi to find work. Stalin provided work.

A lasting contribution to Stalinist architecture is seen in city streetscapes, rather than in a single building. Canal development enabled sewage to be handled separately from the water supply. Buildings along canal embankments became prime real estate, rather than random crowded streets, packed with crowded dwellings for impoverished inhabitants. Streets were widened, and the buildings' housing political, military, and other civic purposes became larger and taller. Stalin era buildings evolved in size along with Soviet bureaucracy. Stalin cities in appearance seem to channel Peter I, without the elegance of Peter's European city design.

Stalin's Indoor Swimming Pool in his Sochi Estate

Stalin's Villa in Sochi

Buildings housing the communist party elite were anything but Spartan. Soviet Socialism evolved from utilitarian communism to include balconies, arches and numerous windows in apartment homes of the elite. Penthouses included bay windows, along with classical columns that appear everywhere. Plaster artistic reliefs identify homes of the upper echelon in an art deco style.

An Architectural Tour of Sochi

Sochi is associated with Stalinist architecture, as Stalin personally directed building efforts while relaxing in Sochi in the early 1930s. Sochi was then, as it is now, the warm weather resort town of Russia. The largest of Stalinist projects, the Palace of the Soviets, was planned for Moscow. The most emblematic of Stalinist architecture, the Red Army Theatre, built in the shape of the Soviet red star, with its flanking colonnades, is in Moscow. Sochi holds a legacy of smaller projects, befitting the smaller city, still outstanding examples of Soviet Realism, outsized for the city.

The central train station of Sochi, seen from the cruise ship pier, has characteristic arches, classical columns, and roof-top obelisks of Stalinist style. Sochi Art Museum, built in 1936, is a historic timepiece. Built toward the beginning of the socialist realism period, the building is smaller in proportion to its oversized portico with massive columns. Optics, not function, exemplify Stalinist architecture.

Appreciation for historic Stalinist architecture was lacking when Olympic fever engulfed modern-day Sochi. Some Stalinist era buildings were lost to Olympic development. Soviet Realism style is not pretty or functional. It may be seen as bullish, overly imposing, lacking in proportion, and inefficient for its use. All of those factors, which make the structures unattractive today, render Stalinist era buildings representative of an era in historical time. History is what it is. Timepieces of history well preserved draw visitors.

Statues of Stalin, once ubiquitous in Soviet Russia, are absent from modern Russia. Boulevards named for Stalin have been renamed. Guides at the Stalin era prison gulags in Siberia blatantly refer to Stalin's purges as genocide of his people. Modern Russia has evolved from the Soviet era.

Classic Soviet apartment buildings are under redevelopment as more attractive complexes. In a grand nod to tourism, and to preserve history, in an ironic twist to the man who was nominated for a world peace prize, never earned or received, Sochi can now boldly preserve Stalinist architecture, nominate itself for World Heritage Site status, and afford visitors a novel view of history. Stalinist architecture can be adored today, as a timepiece, an asset for Sochi.

BATUMI, GEORGIA

(ANCIENT COLCHIS)

Jason and the Golden Fleece in Batumi

A journey through the Black Sea is not complete without the story of Jason and the Golden Fleece. Long before ancient Greeks populated banks of the Black Sea, in 800 to 600 BCE, there were well-established communities on southern shores of the sea. These communities developed over the prior two millennia, as trade came from the Baltic and the Far East, to converge at present-day Odessa, Varna on the Danube, Sinope, and the eastern Black Sea havens of the land of Colchis, the home of the ancient golden fleece and present-day Poti. Pre-Greek inhabitants of the area may have come from as far away as Egypt. They kept out Greeks until the older populations lost vigor and Greeks gained in population, strength as a seafaring people, and resolve to take new land.

Before Greeks battled Trojans for control of the Hellespont, the entrance to the Black Sea, it was the rare adventurer from the Hellenistic world who made it through to the inland ocean. Jason was one of those who ventured. His quest was for gold, and the fame it would bring him back home in Iolcus, a town on the southeast corner of the Greek peninsula, the land of Thessaly. He traveled in a small, single mast and sail, open craft. Fifty heroes of the day aided him to man the oars. Jason's quest, itinerary, and adventures on the way to his goal and back was a magnificent story in his day. That story has been glorified, embellished and gentrified ever since.

Most historians agree that such a quest as Jason's could have occurred before the Trojan wars of 1220 BCE. Parts of his story can be substantiated in the archaeological and historical record. Some believe that Jason was a common pirate in search of booty, who became aggrandized in legend. Others believe that the story of Jason was a compilation of many journeys by several adventurers, mixed with local myths. For the present-day traveler, it can be fascinating to travel along a 3,500year-old itinerary, from Greece, through the Hellespont, to long-established Black Sea ports. Jason, as a myth or reality show, the story still fascinates.

Jason and the Argonauts – Stories of Conquest and Valor

There are several versions of the Jason story.[82] Versions in the earliest records are graphic in gruesome detail. They involve dismembering and human sacrifice. A formalized, enduring tale of Jason comes from Greek historians of the third century BCE. By this time, human sacrifice was not the norm and gruesome details of Medea dismembering her brother to distract her father, so that Jason may escape, are evolved into a heroic sword fight between Jason and her brother, over who shall take Medea home.

The time-honored Greek version is embellished with intermittent tales of the time for travelers. Early twentieth-century Irish poet and playwright Padraic Colum relied on the Greek version to create an English version, which has been popular with adults and children for almost a century. The story here relies in great part on the later, delightful tales of Jason.

This story begins, as so many stories of kings and their domains, with the king of Iolcus and his two sons, Pelias and Æson. Æson was much loved by the people and his father, while Pelias was a man of war; more feared than admired. Æson went into hiding with his wife to escape a worse fate, when Pelias ascended to king of Iolcus. For his safety and education, Æson gave the infant Jason to Chiron, the mythical centaur. The only possession of the infant

---

[82] There are several spellings of the Jason crew and ports along their journey. This story merges spelling from ancient Greek and current scholarship, informed by classic English tales.

was a gold ring with a ruby carved with the face of Æson, so that Jason would know his father when the time came to return to his family.

From Chiron, Jason learned to hunt and to find his way across land. Jason was raised to be strong, although socially naïve. There was only so much a centaur could do to raise a young man. At some point, the inevitable happened. Jason went to Iolcus to see his uncle. On the way there, Jason was aided in crossing a swift stream by a frail older woman, who had the strength to carry him across rapidly moving water. The older woman was likely Hera, the wife of Zeus, and the protector of Jason. When his foot touched the water, the current was so swift that one of his sandals was washed away. Jason hobbled into Iolcus with one sandal and his gold ring.

When Pelias first saw Jason, he was shocked. It was not the familial resemblance that surprised Pelias. Pelias had been to an Oracle who told him that a young man with blue eyes and golden hair would come into his domain wearing one sandal. According to the Oracle, this man would cause the end of the reign of Pelias. Of course, Jason did not know the prophecy.

Pelias welcomed Jason and his family into the palace, where a banquet was held in their honor. In a magnanimous gesture, Pelias assured his relatives a future home in the palace, once Jason returned from his quest for the Golden Fleece, which was to Pelias a death sentence. Jason quickly accepted the challenge to prove his manhood. His father was deeply concerned as he understood what the youth did not. The quest for the Golden Fleece was an unattainable mission that would certainly end in death for Jason.

In another of the seemingly endless fortunate events to surround Jason, a boat builder named Argus appeared to take on the task of building a ship. The center beam of the ship came from the palace roof, which had been an oak tree logged from the forest of Zeus. The ship was named the Argo, and those who sailed with Jason became known as Argonauts.

Fifty heroes signed up to sail with Jason. Jason's former caretaker, the centaur, sent Orpheus. Orpheus was too old to take an oar, but he offered wisdom for the sailors. Tiphys and Nauplius came equipped with knowledge of the wind and the stars. Arcas, wearing a bearskin, and Atlanta, the young woman, trained by Artemis, were oarsmen, who could also hunt for food along the

Medea Holds A Golden Fleece Over the Main Square of Batumi Today

journey. Zetes and Calais were twin grandsons of the king of Athens, fathered by the Northwind, Boreas. The incredibly strong Heracles came with his young friend, Hylas.[83]

Some of the Argonauts appear in later Greek stories as warriors at Troy, or fathers of young warriors who battle at Troy. Nestor was older than most Argonauts, but he appears in tales of the Trojan War as a fighter at Troy. Argonaut Peleus was the father of Achilles, and Argonaut Telamon was the father of Ajax. Their sons were heroes at Troy.

Other Argonauts have a separate place in history. Argonaut Admetus became a king. Argonaut Theseus started the journey by lifting the huge stone indicated by his mother to find the sword of his unnamed father. Theseus joined the Argonauts, hoping to gain acclaim that would cause his father to be disclosed to him. Once Jason returned to Iolcus, Theseus continued his story, which included slaying the Minotaur in the maze on Crete and ended when Theseus became king of Athens.[84]

Other heroes were named in later editions of the Jason story. Historians have counted less than fifty original Argonauts. More heroes were added by local bards to include their favorite home town heroes.

Argonauts were not at sea for long when Heracles broke his oar. They beached in unknown territory, while Heracles went to find a suitable tree from which to carve a replacement oar. Back at the beach, rude men appeared and threatened the Argonauts. Argonaut Polydeuces was challenged to box a larger local man. He took a lucky punch and lowered the local. Other locals picked up clubs and chased after the Argonauts. Just in the nick of time, Heracles came out of the forest, holding an entire tree that he wished to use for his new oar. At the sight of him, the locals scattered. Heracles calmly tore the tree down to size with his bare hands and made his new oar.

---

[83] Heracles is better known as Hercules, certainly a sixth century addition to the story, not to leave out a hero.

[84] Theseus has his own story in Cruise through History Itinerary III Ports of the Eastern Mediterranean.

While Heracles was busy impressing the locals, his friend Hylas wandered off to find water. The water nymphs lured Hylas under the water and smothered him with their kisses. When it was time to leave, no one could find Hylas. Heracles was immobilized with grief. It took some incantations from the gods to get Heracles back on the Argo.

The first reprovisioning stop for the Argo was the island of Lemnos, due east of Iolcus. Only women inhabited the island. Lemnos men brought back young, beautiful girls as captives from a raid in Thrace, southern Greece. Angry Lemnos women killed the men and their captives. In another version of the story, women of Lemnos forgot about Aphrodite, becoming unattractive to their men, so the men left.[85]

---

[85] The idea that the women drove off the men is a Greek addition to the story. Ancient Greeks are well known for being incredulous concerning women governing a country. If women are in charge it must be that they were cursed or prevailed upon

When the Argo approached, women of Lemnos strapped on their husband's armor. They thought the ship was full of Thracians coming to steal their young girls. Fortunately for the Argonauts, an aide to Lemnos Queen Hypsipyle convinced her to let the Argonauts land. Queen Hypsipyle understood that their island would become depopulated, without occasional male tourists. The Argonauts agreed to stay for a while and assist in repopulating the island. Only Heracles remained on the ship to grieve for Hylas.

To enter the Black Sea, the Argonauts had to travel through the perilous Symplegades. The Symplegades was the infamous name for the opening of the straits of the Hellespont, where spring ice flows run forth at about fifteen knots. To Jason, the icy boulders were little moving islands sent to test him. He let loose a pigeon given to him by Queen Hypsipyle and followed the bird. Waves crashing against ice created a thunderous noise and blinding spray. Wherever the pigeon was able to fly, the ship followed.

Just when the Argonauts thought they had overcome their latest test, the sky became dark. The cause of darkness was an annual migration of masses of several types of birds. To protect themselves from pointed feather arrows, rowers covered themselves with their shields, while other Argonauts beat upon the shields with the butt of their swords to create noises that would drive away the birds.[86]

Just before the Argonauts reached Colchis, they heard an anguished cry coming from a mountain in the Caucasus. It was the cry of the Titan god Prometheus, who had angered his equal, Zeus. Prometheus would not let Zeus destroy the race of mortal men, so he gave men the fire needed for their survival. Zeus retaliated by chaining Prometheus to the top of a mountain. Everyday ravens pecked at Prometheus. Heracles could not bear to hear the cries of a

---

by Amazons to rule over men. According to the Greeks, Amazons were women who rode horses, wore armor and hated men. Archaeologists have not located an Amazon land, although there is evidence that on occasion armor-clad women fought with men. People did not ride horses at the time of Jason and Troy. Whenever Greek stories include threatening women, Amazons are the cause.

[86] You can simulate this experience at home. Place a garbage can lid or other large, thin, metal object just above your head, while someone beats upon it with another metal object. The Argonauts were brave, but not too bright.

pious god, so he jumped ship and swam to shore, to release Prometheus from bondage. In other and later stories, Heracles performs a dozen labors to atone for his affront to Zeus. Meanwhile, the Argonauts sailed away.

Abandoning Heracles, Argonauts sailed up the river Phasis to the palace of the king of Colchis, home of the Golden Fleece. The ancient kingdom of Colchis comprised the western half of modern Georgia, on the Black Sea. Batumi is a port on the Black Sea coast of ancient Colchis.

The night before the Argonauts arrived in the land of Colchis, King Æetes had a dream that men arriving on a ship would cause his palace to fall. Jason, too, sensed that he should proceed with caution. Two youths came to the Argo, where it was moored just offshore and identified themselves as sons of Phrixos and the daughter of the king. They told Jason that the king was in fear of Jason, and he should proceed with caution.

Jason came to the palace and beheld a place so grand; it amazed him in its opulence. He was also very impressed with the unmarried daughter of the king, Medea. Jason explained to the king that he came only for the Golden Fleece, and he offered to slay some Sauromataes as payment.

Sauromataes were no myth. They were factual enemies of the people of Colchis, and they presented a real and present danger to the king. The king was not impressed. He preferred to see Jason die and see the same fate for his grandsons, rather than allow the prophesy to come true.

King Æetes told Jason that he had won the land by some fantastic feats and that Jason must duplicate them if he wanted the fleece. Jason was told that he must harness the king's fire-breathing team of bulls and plow an entire field in one day. The seed to be planted was the teeth of dragons. Men would spring from the seed, and Jason was to fight them all. Then Jason could take the fleece and be gone.

Jason knew the gods blessed him, but even he was not so stupid as to think he could pull off the described tasks by himself. Meanwhile, Medea was as concerned for her nephews as she was impressed with Jason. She visited Jason and told him she would help him, but he would owe her eternal loyalty. Jason agreed.

City Monument of Batumi Recalls Ancient Myth

Medea gave Jason a potion to soothe the beasts while he harnessed them. Then he plowed the field, while Theseus tossed out dragon teeth. Just as the king predicted, the ground began to swell. Huge, fully-armed men appeared. As instructed by Medea, Jason heaved a heavy boulder into the mass of seething men. Some were crushed instantly, and the rest thought they had been challenged to see who could toss the rock back. The men fought among themselves for the chance to show their strength. Jason went between the in-fighting men and slew them one-by-one.

King Æetes was angry when he learned that Jason succeeded in his assignment. He refused to tender the fleece. The king planned to burn the Argo that night and have his soldiers kill Jason and his friends. At this point, Medea needed to choose between father and lover. She chose Jason.

Medea led Jason to the tree where the fleece hung from a branch, while she put a spell on the serpent that guarded it. Jason and Medea, along with her nephews and remaining Argonauts, ran for the Argo. Medea's brother, Apsyrtus, pursued them.

The nephews were helpful to Jason. They told him that he could not go back the way he came as it was lined with kingdoms, all friendly to King Æetes. Jason was eager not to face the Symplegades again, or the birds, so he took their advice and headed across the Black Sea to the Danube. The plan was to use a very old map of rivers to navigate back to the sea that flowed into familiar waters.[87]

This time Jason was not so fortunate. As he entered the river, Apsyrtus arrived with the joined forces of several kingdoms to cut off Jason's escape. Jason

---

[87] Such maps actually existed. There were maps used by amber traders to reach the Black Sea from the Baltic, as much as 4,000 years ago. The Argonaut stories trace a route from Danube to the Adriatic Sea and southern Italy.

negotiated with Apsyrtus to leave Medea behind and take just the fleece with him. That night, while Medea sat in a cave trying to decide whether she felt more anger toward Jason or Apsyrtus, Jason appeared to take her with him. At the same time, Apsyrtus had the same idea to short-cut the agreement and take Medea with him. The two men faced off in a sword fight. Jason killed Apsyrtus and rushed back to the Argo with Medea.

When the soldiers with Apsyrtus saw their leader slain, they were so struck by sadness that they founded a city in his honor at the spot where he was cut down. To cut in ancient language was *tomi*. The site of ancient Tomis, now known as Constanta, placed this action on the west coast of the Black Sea. It is probably more likely that the soldiers feared returning to Colchis without the fleece, or Medea, and having only the body of Apsyrtus rather than the lifeless body of Jason to present to the king. Whatever the cause, the soldiers were distracted, and the Argonauts escaped.[88]

The Argo sailed through a maze of rivers and reached the Tyrrhenian Sea, at the bottom of the boot that is Italy. Sirens were singing to the sailors to lure them to the rocks. Orpheus sang louder than the Sirens. Even so, some Argonauts jumped ship and swam to shore. The Argonauts remaining on the ship reached the island of the maidens, the home of Medea's aunt Circe. This was a necessary stop. Medea sought a cleansing from Circe to atone for the death of her brother. Circe told Medea that a woman who knew nothing about spells would give her advice and Medea was to live by it.

Eventually, the Argo reached the land of Phoenicians, where soldiers of Colchis waited for Jason. Jason appealed to the king to let him keep his life and the fleece because he met the terms of the king of Colchis. To him, the king breached the bargain. Jason made a winning argument and he was allowed to rest. The Phoenician queen befriended Medea. Although this queen knew nothing about spells, she urged Medea never again to use enchantment to hurt anyone. This woman was the redeemer foretold by Circe.

---

[88] In an earlier, pre-Greek version of the tale, Medea dismembered her brother at the palace of her father to avoid being followed. The king was distracted by his grief and allowed Jason to escape. They sailed west across the sea.

The Argonauts had a few more adventures, such as being blown into the sands of Libya, before they reached Corinth. There King Creon greeted the Argonauts and warned Jason not to return to Iolcus. King Pelias was rumored to have slain Jason's mother and father and was amassing an army to protect his kingdom. King Creon offered to give the Argonauts due honors and an invitation to stay indefinitely. This king also had a daughter who was sweet and knew nothing about spells. The king hoped that his daughter and Jason would make a nice couple. The Argonauts drifted apart. Theseus went to Athens in search of his father, but that is another story.

Medea was conflicted. She knew she could no longer inflict harmful spells to reach her goals, but she could not tolerate seeing Jason separated from his home in Iolcus. The fleece had not yet come full circle and the curse of Jason's family had not been cleansed.

Medea's inner nature won over. She went to the garden of apples and took some fruit. She spent the evening gathering herbs. She then went to a pool and transformed herself into an old woman. In the morning, a chariot with a team of dragons was at her disposal. She brought out all her demons. It was time to pay a visit to King Pelias.

Medea flew to Iolcus in the chariot of dragons. She hid her ride and went to the palace guards with fragrant apples. Medea told the guards to offer the present to the king and ask for a meeting with him. When the king invited Medea to chat, she offered him youth if he would follow her directions. As a test, the king built a vat and filled it with water. Medea appeared and put an old ram into the vat. The water boiled. Then she put herbs in the vat and pulled out a young ram.

The king was enthralled. He thought all night about how he had everything in his power except youth, and this witch would bring him youth. The next day the king prepared to lie down in the vat of boiling water. Medea gave the king's daughters the potion to sprinkle in the water and left town. The daughters did as instructed. When the king did not rise from the water, the daughters called the palace guards. The king was dead. The soldiers that Pelias had amassed to protect his kingdom ran for the hills.

Art Noveau Architecture of Batumi Portrays Mythical Themes

Back in Corinth, Jason forgot his oath to Medea as King Creon's daughter, Glauce, enthralled him. Medea returned, in her beautiful natural form, to give Jason the good news about Iolcus. She saw the couple together. Medea was angry that she had left her father, killed her brother, and voided the cleansing directed by Circe, all for Jason, who did not seem too appreciative. Medea took foam from the mouths of her dragon steeds and threw it at Glauce. The liquid burned Glauce. She lay dying in the arms of Jason. Jason realized too late that he had been ungrateful.

Jason was famous, but alone. He gathered the remaining Argonauts and sailed to Iolcus. There he claimed the throne, which his father had been deprived. He was known as a great king. The Golden Fleece hung in his palace to inspire other young men.

Jason and Medea – Lessons of Honor and Redemption

In pre-Christian Greece, stories that espouse notions of morality, as well as Old and New Testament biblical allegories, are often found. Themes of punishment for past sins and the cleansing nature of redemption and rebirth can be seen throughout the story of Jason and the Argonauts. The Argonaut saga includes a Garden of Eden, with forbidden apples guarded by serpents, visited by Jason and Medea. There is a little side-tale about the lack of virtue in in-fighting. Loyalty, debts of gratitude, and obligation to the family are prominently featured.

The impetus for Jason's quest for the Golden Fleece goes back to the first story of the fleece. This story began when Jason's great uncle was King Athamas of Iolcus. His queen was Nephele. Their children were Phrixos and Helle. As the stories went, Nephele either died or went into servitude when Athamas made Ino his queen. Ino wanted to rid the kingdom of the first round of children, who might compete for the crown with her progeny, so she plotted to kill them. Ino told the women of the town to roast their planting corn. As a result, there was a great famine in the kingdom. Ino told the king that the only way to end the famine was to sacrifice his children.

Phrixus and Helle were dressed to die when a winged golden ram entered the scene and flew them off to another land. Helle fell off at the straits leading to the Black Sea, which are named for her, the Hellespont. Phrixos made it safely to the land of Colchis. He married the king's daughter. When the ram died a natural death, Phrixos and his bride hung the golden fleece over the mantel.

Acts against children forever stained the Kingdom of Iolcus. If Jason could bring back the fleece, through feats of heroism, he would avenge the wrong done to Phrixos and Helle, and redeem his family honor. Jason was tasked with the burden to atone for the sins of his father's family.

In the story of Jason and the Argonauts as a morality play, when the prodigal son returns, all is forgiven. If he dies for the sins of others, he is a martyr for the cause and becomes part of the eternal story. In the end, Jason returned victorious, but it is not a happy ending. There is always a cost when a benefit is attained from the gods. Tales of ancient Jason endure from the Bible to Disney.

Twentieth Century Argonauts

The route of Jason, as described in various versions of the story, has been verified by archaeologists. Several of the places named have been identified with present-day sites having residents dating to the mid-thirteenth century BCE. Iolcus is present-day Volos, a Greek port city in Thessaly. There is a river Phasis on the southern slope of the Caucasus Mountains, on the east coast of the Black Sea. The possible palace of a king has not been found.

There is a basis in fact for the tale of the fire-breathing bulls. The area on the Phasis River, the present-day city of Poti, Georgia, is a place of pitch and gas flames, leading to petrol deposits. The industrial site is not a cruise port stop. The Greek historian Herodotus recorded that Phasis, now known as Poti, was a city of pitch and burning flame. The cruise port is further north in Batumi.

BatumiFuel Fields Today – Source of Ancient Myth

Sixth century Greeks used the method of taking the hide of a ram, with the wool still attached, to catch gold flecks in the river Phasis, as a long-standing, low-tech method of gold mining. There were likely numerous golden fleeces in ancient times. Today there are residents of the area who will demonstrate the method of laying fleece out flat in shallow water to snag gold bits.

Four thousand years ago, Egyptians and Phoenicians were lured into developing settlements along shores of the Black Sea. Coastal trading stations took part in the fascinating and lucrative trade in beads and spices from the Far East. The ancient amber road came south from Russian and Polish shores of the Baltic Ocean, by way of the Dnieper and Danube rivers. At Tomis and other ancient Black Sea ports, amber was traded for local grain and luxuries from the Far East. Batumi had coal to offer in trade.

Residents of trading settlements on shores of the Black Sea were successful in keeping out Greeks until about the eighth century BCE, when the first Greek settlement on the Black Sea was established at ancient Sinope, a former Phoenician mercantile center. Travelers to the region today can purchase beads, spices, and amber from their distant origins. Inner sea trade has a long history.

In 1977, a modern-day British Jason sought to replicate the journey of the Argonauts.[89] A new Argo was built for twenty oarsmen (and women), to sail from Greece through to the Black Sea. The full trip was a distance of 1500 miles. A great deal of research was done to replicate the 3,000-year-old design of the Argo in each historical detail. The new Argo left from Volos, after several years of planning. Sailors used ancient Greek text, *Argonautica*, to guide their route. They departed on May 3, and arrived at Poti on July 21, to a cheering crowd.

Buoyed by success, the later-day Argonauts replicated several ancient voyages. The voyage of the Argonauts is the oldest and the only historic voyage of note on the Black Sea. Later battles occurred outside the Hellespont, at Troy and Athens. Jason's story provides enduring morality vignettes and a glimpse into early travel to ports of the Black Sea. Travel to those ports today, of Batumi, Sinop (ancient Sinope), and Constanta, among others, remain an adventure. Golden Fleece today is found in sportswear logos and private clubs. Travel to the Black Sea is an enjoyable adventure.

---

[89]   Tim Severin, Jason Voyage, Simon and Shuster, New York, 1985.

Peaceful Batumi City Parks

BATUMI – A LITTLE BIT OF FRANCE IN GEORGIA

The surprise destination for travelers to ports of the Black Sea must be Batumi. Settled before the arrival of Greeks, becoming a destination of Greeks and Romans, the story begins much like other ports of the Black Sea. From Romans forward, the tale of Batumi diverges from the remainder of its neighbors. While northern and southern shores of the Black Sea came under Ottoman Turkish control and either remained Ottoman or, as in the north, became part of Russia and the Soviet Union, Georgia managed to remain a little island of independent royals. It was able to withstand invaders, at least until the twentieth century, when it too became part of the Soviet Union. The last of its royals fled or were executed during the Soviet era.

Georgia stretches from the Black Sea along the southern range of the Caucasus Mountains. In ancient times the western portion on the Black Sea was known as the kingdom of Colchis, fiercely resistant to Greek and Roman settlement. Romans began a settlement, which became Batumi, only to abandon it for Petra, Jordan, and lucrative trade of Arabian seas.

The royal family that developed in Georgia was not Turkish, Slavic, or Russian. Although Georgia aligned with Russia in its history to obtain a strong partner in defending against incursion from Iran. In the nineteenth century, Russian association was a defense against becoming subsumed by the spreading Ottoman Empire. Joseph Stalin was born in Georgia. It was important to him that his birthplace be part of his Soviet Union.

Independent once again, since the collapse of the Soviet Union, Georgia is protective of its unique place between Turkey and Russia. It desires non-hostile, non-allegiance with both neighbors. Tbilisi, the capital, sits well inland, closer to Caspian Sea countries, the Stans, than its Black Sea coastal city of Batumi.

Walking the streets of Batumi today, the visitor is immediately struck by the beauty of a city more European than Euro-Asian. Wide boulevards, lined with palm trees and gracious French-style buildings, look more at home on the French Riviera than the Black Sea. French pirates and French knights came to Batumi, as traders, not conquerors. They made an impression on royals and residents of Batumi, which persisted over time in French connections to this eastern city on the edge of Asia.

Batumi has an ancient history, acknowledged in the statue of Medea, who sits on top of a pillar in the middle of the plaza of the old central city. In all other features, this is a nineteenth to twentieth-century city of planned streets and large, well-built commercial and public buildings, surrounded by apartment towers positioned to take advantage of sea views. Batumi is a European resort city. This is the short story of how Batumi became a little bit of France on the Black Sea.

A Little Georgian History

In the tenth to eleventh centuries, a period known in Europe as the Dark Ages, a royal family was developing in Georgia. The united Georgian Kingdom came to its zenith under King David IV and successor Queen Tamar, known as Queen Tamar the Great. They are not well known outside of Georgia, as Georgia was not often an aggressor country that sent troops to align in war. Monarchs of Georgia sought alliances to remain out of war and still withstand external aggression.

King David ruled from 1089 to 1125. In that time, he kept the kingdom united and kept the Turks from overtaking the area, as they spread southeast into Anatolia, present-day Turkey. In twenty years of almost continual battles, David expanded the kingdom to the Caspian Sea.

David was also known as the builder king. A champion of the Georgian Orthodox Church, he built churches, for which he was canonized. Religion kept the kingdom united over time. Monasteries educated Georgians in the Georgian language and its unique script. Cultural unity was a defense against invasion. The Gelati Monastery, founded by David in 1106, is now a World Heritage Site.

David knew how to use the political power of religion. He was born in 1073, just two decades after the Great Schism divided Catholic Rome from Eastern Orthodox Constantinople. Building churches was not an act of mere altruism. In the break between Georgian neighbor Armenia with Constantinople, Georgia kept close ties with Byzantine Eastern Orthodoxy in Constantinople, which at the time had a more powerful army and a large, successful empire. As head of the church in Georgia, and its favorite son, David had the political/religious heft to make such decisions.

David was succeeded by a son and then daughter Tamar, who ruled from the death of her brother in 1158 to her death in 1161. She was a nun who left the cloister to run the kingdom. Historians give her little credit for her contribution.

The next great leader of Georgia was another Tamar, who was born in 1160, the year before her namesake died. She ruled Georgia from 1178 as regent for her son and then as ruler in her own right from 1184, to her death in 1213. Her coronation was held in Gelati Monastery.

One of King David's Orthodox Churches in Batumi

Historians give Tamar begrudging credit for successful repulsion of further attempts of the Ottoman Turks to invade Georgia. Russian historians glorify Tamar as the king who rode with her troops into battle against Persians and Turks. It was twenty years after her death before another invasion attempt was made. During her reign, the sea frontage on the Caspian Sea expanded. She looms large in Georgian popular culture and arts. Frescos of Tamar are seen in Georgian churches.

Tamar's greatest accomplishment was maintaining her right to rule. Her father designated Tamar as his successor, a designation that court advisors were reticent to accept. They considered her regent for her son, though she was eventually given the title of king. Historians have altered that title in retrospect to be queen, or queen regent. Kings ruled. Queens were appendages.

Tamar's subjects were more accepting. They designated her as great for her strong, calm hand over thirty-five years of rule. She remained head of the Christian monarchy even after she divorced her first husband, an over-ambitious Armenian, whom she exiled to Armenia post-divorce after he made two coup attempts. She was nominated to sainthood during her lifetime, no doubt for her sponsorship of copied religious manuscripts. She and her second husband had two children, thus securing the line of family royals. Her husband appeared on coins as consort to the king, or queen consort and never as king. Canonization records of Tamar identify her as King Tamar.

When Byzantium fell to the Ottoman Turks, who entered Constantinople in 1453, it was a great blow to Georgians. The Georgian Orthodox Church sought ties to Catholic Rome. Ready ties to Europe give clues to the cultural propensity of Georgians.

Throughout the fifteenth and sixteenth centuries, coastal Batumi was attacked by Ottoman forces in an attempt to join Georgia with Ottoman held Turkey and the eastern end of the Mediterranean. Several times Ottoman forces claimed victory, only to see Batumi retaken by imperial Georgia. In 1444, when Ottoman Turks were making their big push at the western coast of the Black Sea to conquer Varna, Batumi experienced an attempted invasion from an unexpected foe.

Graceful Palaisades Line Batumi Streets Today

Geoffroy de Thoisy was a French knight of dubious alliances. Sent to join the Knights of St. John in defense of Christian Varna, he decided that it was the better part of valor to keep his resources for future battles, by waiting out the victor of Varna in safer streets of Constantinople. Looking for some profitable excitement, de Thoisy sailed to Trebizond on the south coast of the Black Sea and engaged in piracy. Then he decided to follow the current east to Batumi, even though the mayor of Trebizond advised him that the people of Georgia were Christian.

The French knight consoled himself in the fact that though Georgians were Christian, they were Orthodox and not Vatican Catholics. As he sailed to new conquests, people of Trebizond sent a warning to Batumi. Waiting for de Thoisy in Batumi were armed soldiers of the king. To his amazement, de Thoisy was ambushed, taken captive, and his men executed. Cooler heads of the Knights of St. John implored the mayor of Trebizond to mediate release of the errant knight. He returned to France, where he became an advisor for future crusade campaigns.

Batumi was finally conquered and made part of the Ottoman Empire in 1723. Islamification of the population began, although, for the most part, it was surface conversion. Within a century, Georgia was joined with Russia and promptly returned to Eastern Orthodoxy, until all religion was banned after 1917, in the socialist era.

Georgian monarchy, displaced by Russian control of the country, fled to Paris. Notably, Prince George Eristavi and his wife Princess Mary became part of the social elite of Paris after they fled Georgia in 1912, in the waning days of the monarchies of Georgia and Russia, as Bolsheviks created havoc in both countries. Princess Mary, born in Batumi in 1888, near the commencement of Russian Imperial control, was a lady-in-waiting to Empress Alexandra Feodorovna of Russia. Mary was regarded as a Georgian beauty, who found work in Paris as a model for Coco Chanel.

While in Paris, Mary was spotted by Georgian poet Galaktion Tabidze, who was besotted with her. He wrote thousands of poems, among them, many dedicated to or written in a rapture of Mary. He returned to Georgia. In the Stalin era, when Tabidze's wife and many associates were sent to Siberia, he became so depressed that he was hospitalized. Tabidze ended his life by jumping from a hospital window. Mary lived to be ninety-eight in Paris. Her life is worthy of a movie.

Art Nouveau Batumi

Europe Square in the French Style City

Building Batumi

The view of Batumi from the port is that of an elegant nineteenth-century European city. The streets are wide and straight, the city square is ringed with large nineteenth to twentieth-century Art Nouveau and Art Deco buildings, in colors of pale pink and blue. The clock tower sits above a spacious shopping plaza, linked to shops by covered, vaulted walkways, where shoppers walk under rosettes and floral reliefs usually seen in grand palaces.

Shortly after Georgia was aligned with Russia in 1878, construction of major infrastructure projects began. Skilled workers and multi-national investors came to Batumi. The Batumi-Tbilisi railway was expanded, and a Baku-Batumi pipe-line brought oil from the fields of Baku to the growing port of Batumi. The Baron Rothschild Caspian and Black Sea Oil Company employed over a thousand workers.[90] Batumi grew rapidly in population from 1883 to the early 1900s.

---

[90]   In 1901, Batumi resident Joseph Stalin organized labor strikes.

The central market square of the city was formalized with paving and augmented by a statue of Medea on a pillar. A theatre built on a separate square has gilded moldings and sits within a formal garden. The large Theatre Square fountain sports a large gilded statue of Neptune. From Neptune Square, there are boulevards to and from the port and to and from the center of town. Buildings along the boulevard are French in style, with Mediterranean arched porticos providing sidewalk shade for coffee bars. Elegant apartment buildings and shops line the street behind rows of palm trees. As though planning for automobile traffic, there are plenty of parking spaces.

Visiting Batumi Today

Further from the port, downtown Batumi opens to the early twentieth century with business towers and hotels. The political capital of Georgia is Tbilisi in the interior. The east coast sits along the Caspian Sea. Batumi is the business and cultural capital of Georgia.

Cruise visitors wander streets in Batumi and take shore excursions further interior to gardens and parks with elaborate fountains, both in classical French style and ultra-modern. Batumi is also a resort city, with large resorts along the coast further away from town, as well as apartment towers in the city, which face the ocean and sport canvas shade awnings for the summer sun.

Batumi is a treat for exploration, with open boulevards, along palm-lined streets. French is the expected language. Tucked into the southeast corner of the Black Sea, Batumi is an island of Europe in an unexpected spot.

TRABZON, TURKEY

(ANCIENT TRAPEZUES)

Sumela Monastery: A Tale of Ecumenical Resilience

Greeks founded Trabzon sometime between the sixth to the eighth century BCE. Their motivation for sailing so far from Athens was food. Greek civilization successfully overpopulated its environment and sought new fields to grow grain. They found an opportunity on the southern shores of the Black Sea. Trabzon grew as a port from which goods brought north to the Black Sea from Persia were joined with locally grown grain and shipped to Greece and other ports of the Eastern Mediterranean. Life in Trabzon was good.

Greeks held a monopoly on trade until Romans became supreme masters of the sea around the beginning of the current/Christian era. The First Roman, Christian emperor, Constantine, enjoyed remaining a distance from the intrigue of Rome. His capital, at the entrance to the Black Sea, was established in the small port of Byzantium. Constantinople, the capital of Byzantium, under Constantine became the capital of the Eastern Roman Empire. Byzantine Christians took control of trade from about 400 to 1400, until Muslim Turks became maters of the sea and took control of access to the Black Sea, which they hold today. While Byzantium lasted, life in Trabzon was good.

Regardless of the economic prowess of Greeks in Trabzon, Greeks maintained a vibrant community there for 2,500 years. Surrounded by growing Muslim communities, Greeks held to Orthodox Christianity and to places where Christianity was preserved. Sumela Monastery, high on a mountain above Trabzon, was one such place. This is the story of resilience in this special place. When life was good, the monastery expanded. When life was suspended, the cluster of buildings, containing a wealth of Byzantine art in fresco, was ignored. Isolation enabled preservation.

Sumela – The First 1600 Years

The Sumela Monastery sits high on a mountain anchored as though it grew out of a large cave. This cave was a shelter to early people, who preceded Greek colonists. Who these people were and whether they used the cave for ceremonial purposes is left to historical speculation. Several legends mark Sumela cave as a holy place. There is no evidence left today of pagan practice.

Legends of Trabzon include the story of an icon of the Virgin Mary painted by Saint Luke, disciple of Jesus Christ. The icon, a classic Byzantine Orthodox painting on a block of wood, was several inches square. Upon the death of Luke, unknown persons sent the icon to Athens. Then a miracle occurred in the fourth century when the icon was spirited away from Athens by angels. The angels deposited the icon in a cave high above Trabzon, where it rested untouched for years.

Two Greek priests of Athens, who were hermit monks, were ambling through the area of Trabzon when they spotted the icon in the cave. The year was 386 CE, and the monks making the fortuitous find were Barnabas and Sophronios.

They appealed for support to Roman Emperor Theodosius, known to be generous in matters of Christianity. Funded by Theodosius, they founded Sumela Monastery.[91]

The original monastery was a rock church within the high cave. Walls of the cave were deepened and smoothed, then painted completely with frescoes depicting cosmos of the early church. A straight wall was built across the entrance. Two hundred years later, this site of many pilgrimages was restored and expanded by another Byzantinian emperor, Justinian.

---

[91] There is no evidence for the story of the founding of Sumela Monastery, other than legend. The monks from Athens may have assisted the angels to bring the icon to Turkey. http://www.goturkey.com/content.php?cid=51578&typ=c&lng=en Last visited 5/30/12. Faith needs no proof. Theodosius was the host of the Council of Nicaea, from which came the Nicaean Creed, making Arianism heretical. Galla Placidia, daughter of Theodosius was held captive and later married the Arian leader of the Goths, who sacked Rome and carried away Galla. See more on Galla in Cruise through History, itinerary II – Port of Ravenna.

The monastery supported itself by selling small icons, replicas of the icon of the Virgin Mary, as painted by Saint Luke. Pilgrims came to feel the healing powers of the Virgin and to bathe in the sacred pool of water in the cave. The pool was fed by clear water, percolating through rock, which dripped from the ceiling into a font.

Historians have tried to discern the origin of the name of the monastery. In the Greek language, Sumela means dark or black. Since the monastery was founded on the site of the icon, the name may refer to a Black Madonna. A historian visiting the monastery in 1840, while it was still in full operation, noted the sacred icon was indeed very dark. Photographs taken of the icon show a split piece of wood, with no discernible picture, in an eighteenth-century frame. Whether the visitor saw the ancient original or a more recent copy, it was evident that the artist intended the portrait to be dark, or that mold darkened the image over time in the damp cave.

Black Madonna depictions were common in Eastern Europe. They are also found in remote mountain villages in France, such as Rocamadour, in southwestern France. French Chapelle de Notre-Dame is an eleventh-century

Fresco in the oldest section of Sumela Monastery
showing layers of art left after removal of frescos

cliff castle, with a prominent black icon figure. Black icons are associated with healing, and the black paint is intended to emphasize a mysterious expression. Since the Sumela Monastery dates to the fourth century, it is possible that the Black Madonna of Sumela was an inspiration for Madonnas throughout Western and Eastern Europe.

There is no doubt that Sumela Monastery was famous throughout the Christian world. It was the object of many pilgrimages. Souvenir icons from Sumela were widely dispersed. Other monasteries were built in the area of Trabzon, none more dominant than Sumela. In Sumela, the sick could be healed by standing under its rock ceiling to imbibe in drops of miraculous water.

Sumela was fortunate to have a powerful patron in the fourteenth century. In 1261, the powerful Komnenos Dynasty took control of the Byzantine Empire. Their capital was Trabzon. Alexios Komnenos III, who headed the dynasty from the mid-century to 1390, was saved from a storm at sea by his belief in the Virgin Mary. His father and grandfather had supported Sumela Monastery, so Alexios felt his contribution to the faith in thanks for survival was to expand the monastery.

Alexios built a chapel next to the rock church. A kitchen area and living quarters for monks were constructed. Storage rooms were added, one of which became the monastery archive. Several large structures, the remnants of which can be seen today, date to the time of Alexios. As the Komnenos dynasty began to lose power, at the beginning of the fifteenth century, the family gave substantial sums to Sumela Monastery to ensure its continued well-being. Patronage was not entirely gratuitous. Often monarchs looked to monasteries, funded in good times, as places of royal refuge in troublesome times, or as retirement enclaves.

Ottoman Sultan Mehmed II[92] conquered the Byzantine Empire in 1453, pushing Christians from control of the Black Sea region. He took control of Trabzon in 1461. Instead of imposing Muslim doctrine on Sumela and other monasteries, Mehmed gave them protection. He issued a formal decree

---

[92] Mehmed is sometimes written Mehmet or Mohamad. Mehmed II's father, Murad II led the 1444 Battle of Varna.

protecting the ancient rights of Sumela Monastery. Eight successive sultans did the same. The Virgin Mary was regarded throughout Turkey as a source of healing. Sultans regarded Sumela Monastery as the key place to commune with the spirit of the Virgin.[93]

Evidence of Ottoman control of Trabzon is seen in the monastery. Turkish iconoclastic art and design in fresco were added to the monastery interior, seen in fireplaces and cupboards. In some places, there are three layers of frescos. Frescos were added from the fourteenth to the eighteenth century. Unfortunately, some later frescos were removed by twentieth-century relic hunters, damaging underlying older frescos.

The largest building at Sumela, the imposing, often photographed, iconic appearance of Sumela, seen from a distance on the hillside, was built in 1840. Early to the late nineteenth century was the time of highest occupancy and use at Sumela. The three-story building, with small windows and a wooden roof, housed monks and guests. There were frequent guests at Sumela.

---

[93] Four major prophets of Islam are Abraham, Moses, Jesus and Mohamed.

As monks traveled across Turkey, the Balkans, Russia, and surrounding areas selling icons from Sumela, there was sustained interest in pilgrimages. Donations came to Sumela, enabling construction of wooden balconies and decorative carving around the inner courtyard. Visitors from England and Europe traveled to Sumela, including journalists, historians and photographers. Much is known of Sumela from this time due to records of its fame throughout the western world.

At its height, Sumela Monastery was a rambling, extensive complex on five levels. The dormitory had seventy-two rooms for monks and guests. Building interiors and exteriors were largely covered in frescos and paintings. The latest buildings date to construction in 1860. Water was brought into the complex by an aqueduct running along the mountainside and near steps to the monastery entrance. There was a room for a doorkeeper under an arch that was lost in a fire.

Access to Sumela has always been an athletic venture. It was reached from Trabzon by a steep path through the forest. Today there is a parking lot close to the base of the mountain. Visitors are treated to a lovely walk in the forest, over tree roots and rocks, until monastery buildings break with

the natural environment. The complex is entered after climbing a steep set of narrow stairs. Only then, does the visitor step down into the main courtyard, to receive a view of the assembled buildings, emanating from rock, adjoined by free-standing room blocks added over centuries.

Upon descending into the courtyard, the visitors' first view is the impressive rock church, seen to the left. The ancient sacred spring was deep inside the church, within the cave. Outside the rock church was a fountain, a later addition, to collect water from the spring. Surrounding the courtyard, buildings added over time randomly were connected in the nineteenth century by walkways and balconies. To the right of the entrance platform, the largest building beyond the cave was the living quarters for monks and numerous guest rooms. The most important building in the large dormitory structure was the library, where records of Sumela were carefully stored, together with important documents issued by kings and sultans granting exclusivity of use and exemption from taxation.

By the end of the nineteenth century, Sumela Monastery was an imposing place. It was a point of destination for pilgrims and adventurous travelers. At the beginning of the twentieth century, the inhabitants of Sumela began to be impacted by politics of the city below, which encroached on their activities. Then in 1916, Russians invaded Trabzon. For almost two years, it appeared that Russia would take permanent control of the area and bring the Eastern Orthodox Christian state back to Trabzon. Russia's internal political struggles and the War of National Liberation that brought independence to Turkey, dashed any hopes of Sumela existing in a Christian nation. With the wars came a reduction of visitors and of income necessary to maintain the monastery.

Sumela – The Power of Place

In 1923, after almost 1600 years of constant habitation and use, Sumela Monastery was abandoned. Abandonment was not voluntary. In that year, the Ottoman Empire in Turkey came to an end. The Turkish Republic was built on a theme of separation of church and state. It was Turkish leader Ataturk's vision to move Turkey into the Twentieth Century, by releasing government from the bounds of religious dictates. Progress did not include religious freedom, or toleration.

In the new Turkey, Sumela Monastery no longer received government protection. In 1923, Christian Greece and Muslim Turkey agreed in the Treaty of Lausanne to resolve their differences by expulsion of ethnic Turkish Muslims from Greece and ethnic Greek Christians from Turkey. From Trabzon alone, 100,000 Greeks, whose ancestors had lived in the area for over 2,500 years, were loaded onto ships sailing for Athens.[94] In just days, Sumela Monastery and its supporting Christian community were depopulated. Sumela was deserted.

In 1930, Sumela monastery, lacking a loyal resident population, suffered a fire. The devastation was extensive to all wooden parts of the monastery complex. The wreckage became a haven for vandals. Fortunately, some of the movable objects left Turkey with Sumela monks, ensuring preservation. Frescos on walls that survived the fire were not so fortunate. Centuries-old frescos appear to have been cut from stone walls by experts after the fire. Recovered frescos were for international covert private sale, rather than preservation as a cultural legacy. Sumela Monastery sat in a foreign land, where it was not considered part of historic, cultural, or religious heritage.

The legend of a hidden treasure of Sumela artifacts began as departing monks were not allowed to take anything with them from Sumela upon departing in 1923. Fearing looting or destruction of their icons, monks hurriedly buried what they could. Over the years, and certainly, after the 1930 fire left the place exposed, adventurous monks returned secretly to Sumela to retrieve buried items. As a result, some items from the original Sumela Monastery in Turkey can now be found in the new Soumela Monastery, on another mountain, Mount Vermio, near Naousa in Macedonia, Greece. Naousa is where some monks of Sumela made their new home.

Other artifacts from Sumela, including documents from the library, have gone to several institutions. Most of the library manuscripts are in the Turkish

---

[94] In similar fashion, Muslims in Greece were forced to sail for Istanbul. Muslims from Greece in Istanbul, and Greek Christians from Trabzon in Athens, were without support mechanisms once they arrived in new surroundings. They were ethnically the same, but culturally diverse, from their new neighbors, having derived from ancestors who lived for hundreds or thousands of years in their country of expulsion. Many died of hunger and disease. The Treaty of Lausanne was an experiment to attempt peace by ethnic cleansing. It failed to end ethnic tensions.

National Museum in Ankara. Religious texts and icons from Sumela are found in the Hagia Sophia Museum in Istanbul. Other objects are in the Museum of Byzantine Works in Athens. The sacred icon of the monastery is in the National Gallery in Dublin. Prized silver candlesticks, a gift of Sultan Selim, were stolen in 1877, and the location is unknown. Other items are in private collections.[95]

On August 15, 2010, an Orthodox Catholic mass was held at Sumela Monastery for the first time in eighty-seven years. The mass was held with the permission of the Turkish government.[96] Using a special permit issued by the Ecumenical Patriarchate of Constantinople, up to five hundred visitors were allowed in the Sumela Monastery to celebrate the Assumption of Mary.[97]

---

[95] http://www.kultur.gov.tr/EN,32834/sumela-monastery.html. Page 3. Last visited 5/30/12

[96] http://www.sumela.com Last visited 5/30/2012.

[97] Using 21st century technology, the mass at Sumela was broadcast to a nearby café, where it was shown on big screen television to another crowd.

In 2012, the Turkish government began funding restoration work at Sumela Monastery. Tourism to the monastery has been growing. Many who enjoy a pilgrimage to Sumela are from Russia and Greece, keeping alive millennium-old traditions.

Conscientious tourists may have concerns about the impact of their visitation on fragile places of history. At Sumela Monastery, enthusiasm for visitation is what currently drives its preservation. Visitors may enjoy this peaceful place of reflection that has remained intact, high above religious and political changes occurring in the landscape below.

SINOP, TURKEY
(ANCIENT SINOPE)

Sinop Fortress Prison of Freedom's Poet – Sabahattin Ali

There are a few vestiges of early Greek and Roman life at the ports of the southern shores of the Black Sea. The fortress-prison at the water's edge in Sinope, now Sinop, is one of them. As a fortress, the rock structure held a commanding position overlooking boat traffic from Trebizon, now Trabzon, to the east, at the head of roads to Persia and Constantinople, for over a millennium. As a prison, the block and plaster fortress held twentieth-century writers, poets and journalists, who were all political dissidents.

Built in the seventh century BCE, the fortress-prison was closed in 1997. Two years later, the site was turned over to the Culture and Tourism Ministry. Today it is visited by hundreds of thousands of tourists annually, mostly Turks, who understand the significance of the place.

There are two stories of the Sinop Fortress Prison: The history of the building and development of the site as it was continually utilized over 2,700 years, and the story of a famous recent resident, Sabahattin Ali. Today as the visitor walks along dank, tight, rock corridors, built before the time of Christ, it may be hard to imagine that just eighty years ago, a man now regarded as a leading Turkish poet and author was imprisoned there. These walls have held ancient Greek and Roman soldiers, imprisoned pirates, and a twentieth century man, whose weapon was pen and paper.

The Enduring Greek Fortress

The Cape of Sinop forms a small natural harbor for sea traffic on the south coast of the Black Sea. Greeks founded a colony here in 700 BCE, called Sinope. They were not the first residents. Previously, a city of Miletus sponsored people existed at the site. Miletus, a powerful city on the west coast of Turkey, trading partner with Troy and Ephesus, had outposts on islands of the Aegean. People from Miletus islands likely came for more space, fishing, and some commerce, as did later Greeks. When the Greeks arrived, they protected their interests by building a wall above the sea. Building cities gave Greeks an advantage over nomadic groups.

As waves of new owners over time controlled the fortress, they improved and expanded the site. Persians came up from the south and west from Trebizon. Romans came and expelled Persians. Then early Byzantine Christians became the landlords. In 72 BCE, between Persian and Roman control of Sinope, the Pontus King Mithridates made most of the structural changes that defined the outer shape of the fortress for the next 2,000 years.[98]

---

[98] The traveler may remember Mithridates (also Mithradates) from other stories. He is the ruler who came from the Pontus Mountains, southeast of the Black Sea and

The fortress of Sinop is a standing time capsule of the succession of civilizations dominant in the Black Sea over thousands of years. In the early thirteenth century CE, Turks, who arrived from the east, pushed back Byzantine Christians and began to form the country we know today as Turkey. The north-south wall within the fortress dates to this period. An east-west wall was later installed by Turks, which gave the site the configuration seen today. The tall stone tower on the water dates to the twelfth century.

When building the walls, the Turks made use of whatever was lying around from prior landlords. Look closely at the walls today. In addition to stones, there are cut sections of former Greek and Roman columns and bits of sculpture from ancient temples embedded in the walls.

---

north of the lands of Persia. He was a ruthless ruler, having learned from the Romans to take no prisoners and have no mercy. Romans murdered his father. Mithridates then murdered his mother and brother to take control of the throne and waged war for about 25 years with the Romans to avenge the death of his father. Upon his death, Romans stepped in his domain — for a while.

Early Turks of disparate bands were unable to hold together a vast country with no infrastructure. They were easily subsumed into the Ottoman Turkish Empire that swept in from the steppes of Asia. Ottoman dynasties controlled the Tatars of the north Black Sea and the Turks on the south, combining them into one great empire. Ottoman sultans then looked toward Europe to entertain their consuming passion for control over larger domains.

The house of Osman, recognized as the first great leader in what became the Ottoman Empire, maintained control of much of the Black Sea area and surrounding territories from the fifteenth to the eighteenth centuries. Their victory in the Battle of Varna in 1444, and conquest of Constantinople in 1453, cemented control of an empire that was strong for four hundred years. It became extinct, as did the Romanov dynasty of Russia and the Holy Roman Emperor of Austria-Hungary, in the aftermath of the First World War.

During Ottoman control, Sinope fortress was used to protect the harbor. Boats were moored in sight of guards perched high on fortress walls of the towers above the water. The tower on the calm harborside is immediately in sight of cruise ships today. Another tower sits over the beach. At its height as a fortress, there were eleven watchtowers. Stones from crumbling towers were repurposed to later walls and buildings.

It was during the Ottoman period that part of the fortress was first utilized as a prison. The first records of prisoners held in the fortress occurred in the mid-sixteenth century. The accommodations could be best described as a dungeon. Stone walls and vaulted arches of the first prison sit as crumpled archaeological sites around the more recent block and stucco prison. Stones from older buildings were repurposed into walls and as foundations for new buildings. In its current state, the Fortress Prison is an open-air museum of Sinop political history.

The prison within the old fortress site seen today opened in 1887. Cell blocks and open, cement prison yards are built of stone and cement block, covered in stucco. Plumbing is sparse. It appears that for over the century that the prison was in active use, little maintenance was undertaken.

In 1939, a cell block was added for a juvenile prison. Over time some prison workshops were instituted; however, most prisoners were left to stare at the walls. Sinope Fortress Prison was an active facility until it was closed in 1997. Two years later, it was turned over to the Culture and Tourism Ministry. Most tourists are Turks, curious to see inside the notorious prison.

The Sinope fortress prison was typical of what has been depicted in movies and horror novels. The site has been used several times as a movie set.[99] Picture high stone walls, dark, dank chambers, and men left to die while hanging from chains attached to the walls. The Sinope prison has been described as a place so wet and musty that it was impossible to light a match inside.

In its one hundred ten years in operation, Sinope Fortress Prison housed violent criminals and political prisoners. It was a maximum-security facility from which few were released while still alive. During the last years of the Ottoman Empire, deposed politicians were conveniently stored in the prison. In the early years of modern Turkey, while communism was spreading from Russia to what would become the Union of Soviet Socialist Republics, Turkey kept communist organizers in Sinope Fortress Prison.

This would seem the least attractive place to pass the time if the prisoner was a writer or a poet. Yet in the twentieth century, this maximum security, stone bastion, with dark individual cells and twisted iron bars, looking out on stone walls, was where the emerging Turkish regime-held poets, writers and journalists. Political prisoners included those thought to be a threat to regime stability, by stoking passions of freedom and enraging hardline old believers, even when views of writers were not treasonous.

Listed among the literary prisoners was Nâzim Hikmet, a poet, playwright, and novelist, imprisoned in the 1940s for communist views.[100] Hikmet spent time in several Turkish prisons until he went to Russia, where he died at age sixty-one in Moscow in 1963. Unknown by name in the United States, Hikmet served in the Turkish Navy during World War I, wrote inspirational revolutionary poetry at the request of Atatürk, learned tenants of communism and became enamored with Lenin while in Batumi in 1922, causing his rift with Turkish politicians and landing him in prison. In 1950, Hikmet received a World Peace Prize along with Pablo Picasso and Pablo Neruda. American folk singer Pete Seeger credits Hikmet's poetry with inspiring his lyrics in the 1960s.

---

[99] Turkish movies and television shows filmed at the site are: Firar (Prison Break) (1993); Pardon (Excuse Me!) (2004); and Köpek (The Dog) (2005).

[100] Nâzim Hikmet was born in Salonica in 1902, to an official of the Ottoman regime and a Polish socialite, attended a naval academy at fifteen, and died in Moscow in 1963.

Another prisoner sent to Sinop for inflaming passions of the democratic government of Atatürk, was a young Sabahattin Ali. Ironically, he was sent to prison by Atatürk.

Fortress Prison of Turkish Poet, Sabahattin Ali

Sabahattin Ali was born in 1907, in a town on the western edge of the last vestiges of the Ottoman Empire. It was a historically Greek area, now part of Bulgaria. He lived most of his young life in Istanbul, where he went to school. He graduated in 1926, at age nineteen, and taught for a year in Turkey.

Recognized as a bright young man, Ali was given a fellowship to study in Germany. He returned to Turkey in 1930, at age twenty-three, and taught German in Turkish high schools. In addition to teaching, Ali continued writing poetry.

It was difficult to be an intellectual and expressive free thinker in Turkey during the 1930s. Looking at Turkey from a distance in 1930, it might have seemed that the state would herald democratic thinking. This was the time of the rise of Turkish leader Mustafa Kemal Pasha, later known as Atatürk, the father of modern Turkey.

Sinop Prison Cell of Sabahattin Ali

12th century fortress tower in the port of Sinope

The Kemalists, as Atatürk's followers were known, were determined that Turkey be a leading power in the twentieth century of world commerce. To do so, the Turkish government needed to be secular. The idea of separation of church and state, or mosque and state as the case was, was a bold step for a country with one foot in Europe, seeking to move forward and one foot in Asia, entrenched in fifteenth-century tradition. Atatürk outlawed the fez as an official garment of government employees. Officials were expected to dress like western counterparts.

Changing an entire body politic of centuries in one decade was a substantial task. Kemalists knew that Muslim fundamentalists were one perceived insult from a riot at all times. Keeping the peace in a government in transition is always a difficult business and never more so than for Turkey moving from Ottoman autocracy to democracy. As a left-wing writer and teacher, Sabahattin Ali was caught within a country that allowed him to think freely, but could not afford for him to express himself publicly.[101]

During the time that Ali was teaching, in his early twenties, he and a friend published a humor magazine, Marko Paşa. Some of his poems appearing in

---

[101]   See generally, Muammer Kaylan, The Kemalists, Prometheus Books, Amherst, New York, 2005.

the magazine criticized Atatürk's policies and poked fun at other writers. Ali was arrested for libel and sentenced to jail in Sinope Fortress Prison.

While in jail, Ali continued to write. The humor magazine was published under the names of Dead Paşa, and You Know Who Paşa and Ali Baba. Only youthful exuberance could sustain his writing from the darkness of Sinop. Some of his fellow prisoners were other writers, poets and journalists.

Ali was released from prison in 1933, as part of an amnesty in celebration of the Tenth Anniversary of the declaration of the Republic of Turkey. He returned to teaching, once he proved his allegiance to the regime by writing a poem complimentary of Atatürk.[102] Ali was always closely watched.

Ali had a somewhat normal life for ten years, from 1934 to 1944. During this time, he married and performed his military service obligation. He never stopped writing. Some of his work, the short stories: *Windmill* (1935), *The Ox-Cart* (1936) and the *Voice* (1937), and then the novels, *The Devil Inside Us* (1940), and *Madonna With a Fur Coat* (1943) crossed the line in the eyes of the Kemalist administration.

The 1943 novel, *Madonna in a Fur Coat*, was released in English in 2017 by Penguin Classics, opening up a new generation and broad field of readers. In the story, a young Turkish artist goes to Berlin in the 1930s. He is enthralled by a painting of a woman in a fur coat seen in a gallery. When he meets the woman in the painting, the artist develops an intense relationship, where she, the free-thinking woman, is the male role type and he takes the role of subservient woman. The imagery and writing talent of Ali has been compared to famous classics of England and the US.

Other works of Ali were better known during his lifetime in tattered copies passed among friends. *Madonna in a Fur Coat* follows the exploits of a man despondent, alone, traveling to Berlin in the 1930s, just as Ali traveled to the city at that time. He returned to Turkey with books unavailable in Turkey. He returned to teaching full of enthusiasm. The bright young poet was charged with poisoning the minds of his students and was sent to prison. He was told he would never again be allowed to teach.

---

[102]   "Benim Aşkim," (My Love or My Passion).

Inside the prison of Sabahattin Ali

Sinope Seashore

In 1944, Ali was again imprisoned for a short period of time. Upon release, he was unable to receive a passport. He was also under financial stress as the government limited his ability to earn a living first by teaching and then restricting his work in publishing periodicals. His novels and short stories could not be published in Turkey, eliminating further earnings.

In 1948, at the age of forty-one, Sabahattin Ali tried to cross the border into Bulgaria. It is undisputed that he died at the border crossing. There are several stories as to how he died. Some historians believe that the person hired to take him across the border killed him. He may have been hit in the head with a piece of firewood, and he may have been apprehended by guards at the border and died during interrogation.

The man whose stories were made into movies by Turkish national television during his lifetime, died alone, in an obscure border crossing. Reports of his last moments were controlled by the government. Friends, family, and admirers suspect the government was involved in Ali's demise. The man convicted of the murder of Ali served briefly in prison before being released, fueling conspiracy theories.

In recent years, there have been symposiums to celebrate the works of Sabahattin Ali. When he was not published in Turkey, his books were widely sold in Bulgaria, which claims him as a native son. As Ali's work is translated into other languages, it continues to be read, with renewed popularity.

The prison where Sabahattin Ali spent time as a young man, and no doubt impacted his thinking and writing, is open to visitors. Walking the Sinope Fortress Prison grounds today is an experience in 2,700 years of human history. Visiting the cell where Ali spent most of his time in prison is chilling. The small, dark cell for individual confinement, has one small barred window that looks out at a stone wall, just a few feet from the window. There is no insulation to keep the cell occupant from freezing in winter and becoming unbearably hot in summer. Any paper kept by Ali while in prison would quickly mold. Writing while in prison kept Ali from going insane.

Today in Sinop, Diogenes, who searched for an honest man, has his statue among flowers just outside the Sinope Fortress Prison walls. Diogenes was a Greek, born in 404 BCE in Sinope, Sinop today. He wandered the world of the Black and Aegean Seas until his death in 323 BCE in Corinth. Always the cynic, Diogenes went looking for an honest man, never expecting to find one.

Like Ali, Diogenes was imprisoned for periods of time, wrote tirades and admiration odes to his political leader, who, in the case of Diogenes was Alexander the Great, and sparred with contemporary thinkers, including Plato and Socrates. His cause of death is uncertain. When living in a jar in Corinth, he told onlookers they could throw his lifeless body to the dogs when dead.

No written works of Diogenes have survived. His thoughts are known as recorded by others. The works of Sabahattin Ali survive to extend his influence decades after his death. Expect no statue to Ali in Sinop. The greatest tribute to a man of literature is the continued popularity of his work.

Interior of the Hagia Sophia as a Mosque

Blue Mosque see from the Sultan's Garden Istanbul

ISTANBUL, TURKEY

(CONSTANTINOPLE, BYZANTIUM, CHALCEDON)

Mosques of Istanbul

Domes of the Pigeon Mosque

Majestic would describe the first views of Istanbul from the deck of a cruise ship sailing up the Bosporus. This the waterway that divides Europe and Asia. Istanbul encompasses both sides of the Golden Horn, the inlet from the Bosporus that divides the city. Count the minarets. There is no doubt that Istanbul, not the capital of Turkey today, was from 1453 to World War I, the capital of the Ottoman Empire. Throughout the empire, Ottomans built mosques. No Ottoman city holds as many mosques, of such grandeur, in such density of architectural monuments as Istanbul.

The Ottomans were not the first builders of great mosques. The Qur'an mentions three significant mosques in Mecca and Jerusalem that were dedicated to the Prophet Abraham. These were masjid, a place of prostration for prayer. In Mecca, the Masjid al-Haram, most sacred mosque, is an open-air courtyard, surrounded by a columned portico. In the center is the Kaaba, the most sacred shrine. Only Muslims may enter Mecca. Only those on Hajj, the pilgrimage, may enter the mosque. Very few men may enter the shrine. The Kaaba shrine is truly the house of God, built by Abraham. It is toward the Kaaba that Muslims must face in daily prayers.

The first mosque of Islam is considered the house of the Prophet Muhammad. All subsequent mosques look to the first mosque to replicate its features. The seventh-century house of the Prophet was an Arab house with a large courtyard, which was surrounded by rooms. A portico around the courtyard was supported by columns of wood or stone. Water for the household came from an exterior fountain. Throughout the world, the basic architectural features of the first mosque are replicated, whether built of mud-brick in Africa, or marble in Casablanca.

Mosque architecture is a specialized genre of building today. The Hassan II Mosque of Casablanca, Morocco, the largest mosque in Africa, sits elegantly on the edge of the ocean. Its arcades and columned porticos are of stunning white and green marble. The World Heritage Site mosques of Timbuktu are low profile, mud-brick structures, reinforced by protruding wood.

Mosques of Istanbul form a unique style of mosque architecture described as the Ottoman Mosque style. The basic components of a mosque are present, in large, bold, grandeur, like the empire builders who financed construction. The extended mosque complex, including a school, hospital, or kitchen, reflects the needs of the community served by the mosque. The buildings are iconic in Istanbul.

Fountain of Sultan Mahmud Istanbul 1740

Most mosques in Istanbul were built over a span of two centuries, designed by a small cadre of men, well-schooled in mathematics, Islam and construction. In architecture, form follows function. In Istanbul, the function is dictated by religion, custom and social rules.

This is a short tour through mosques of Istanbul, their component features, the men who built them, and the stories of construction. Each of the mosques was built to commemorate an event, or a person, by sultans, or their mothers. Though they appear similar from a distance, each Mosque is unique. This is a story of the mosques, their secrets, and meanings they hold today.

Masjid Becomes a Mosque

Every mosque begins with a masjid, the place of prostration for prayer. Other components of mosques have developed from religious requirement, practical necessity, or aesthetic appeal. The prayer hall must be large enough to fit all the men of the city. In Istanbul, where there is a large, concentrated population, new mosques were built in neighborhoods as the city grew.

Hagia Sofia Church/Ayasofya Mosque

The first mosque in Istanbul was the Hagia Sofia, a church. It is not unusual to see churches repurposed to mosques. In the absence of a Christian congregation, or upon conquest by Ottomans of a former Christian town, the church, removed of iconography, with the addition of a minaret, easily became a mosque. Eastern Orthodox churches have no pews, which facilitated transformation across the former Byzantine, Eastern Orthodox Empire, as the Ottoman Turks came west to consume former Byzantine territory. In 1453, Constantinople was taken and became Istanbul. The Hagia Sofia Church became the Ayasofya Mosque.

Mosques are devoid of iconography. They contain only geometric designs and calligraphy. When occupying the Hagia Sophia, the Ottomans covered the abundant mosaics with plaster, which preserved them. When the church to mosque became a museum, as it is today, the plaster was removed to reveal golden mosaics of Roman Emperor Constantine, Empress Zoe, and Christ.

Interior of the Hagia Sophia

Obliteration of faces, seen so often in churches and monasteries in the former Byzantine world, was not the work of conquering Muslims. Throughout 726 to 843, there were periods in the history of the Orthodox Christian Church, when iconoclasts reigned. Zealots initially focused upon destroying pagan statues, legacies of the former Greek and Roman era, then turned to deface representations of saints and others seen in tile or fresco on walls of churches and monasteries. The damage is historic and irreparable.

When the Hagia Sofia was opened as a museum in 1935, the mosaics were uncovered, the calligraphy and minarets remained. Movable furniture and carpets were removed. Lighting remained as it was in the Ottoman era. The structure built and rebuilt twice, by 532, remains a true timepiece of the height of the Byzantine Empire. In 532, Emperor Justinian spent 300,000 gold pounds, which is $400 million today, to build the church destroyed by fire in riots, which spilled over from a sporting event.[103]

---

[103] Read about the Nika Riots of the Greens versus the Blues in Cruise through History© Itinerary III Port of Istanbul.

◄ *Interior of the Hagia Sophia*

The first church was built by Roman Emperor Constantine in 337, of wood and stone. Since Constantine was the first Christian emperor, there were no models for him of what a church should look like. Jesus preached in Synagogues. His apostles preached on the steps of pagan temples. Constantine kept the idea of a congregation, facing the priest, who stood at the altar.

For the architectural concept of a church, Constantine looked to the democratic Roman structure of a basilica. A basilica was a meeting hall, a place for the commodities exchange market and law courts. It was an oblong building with a center aisle leading to an apse, the raised area. On the raised area, there were chairs in a semicircle, where speakers could discuss matters and be open to those seated, or standing along the aisles. The bishop's throne was not a democratic concept found in a basilica. It came later in the Christian era.

Constantine placed the Hagia Sophia in a commanding spot in his new city. Completion of the church was left to his son Constantine II, who dedicated the new home of the Orthodox patriarch in 360. The commanding structure that stuns visitors today was the result of the effort of Emperor Justinian, completed in 537, after two former structures burned. The first church burned in 415, and the Nika Riot claimed the second structure, along with most of Constantinople in 532.

Perhaps Justinian put so much effort into the third iteration of the Hagia Sophia, because he wished to overcome the effect of the Nika Riots. Justinian succeeded in building a church that was the largest house of prayer for the next millennium.[104] Its golden dome inspired the faithful, converts, and visitors, who could swear that the sun came down to kiss the gold lid of the church.

To build the church, Justinian called upon Isidore of Miletus and Anthemius of Tralles. Miletus, a sister city of ancient Troy and Ephesus, was later destroyed, but its reputation for great builders remained. Isidore and Anthemius were mathematicians. They were not architects. They knew how to measure the size of a structure and then determine the amount of material necessary to accomplish the feat. They also knew how to assemble, train, and manage the

---

[104] The next church to compete with the Hagia Sophia in size was the Seville Cathedral completed in 1520.

army of workers necessary to build such a major edifice. Seen from the Bosporus today, the Hagia Sophia is a massive undertaking in brick and plaster.

Justinian retained the Constantine model for the church. He enlarged the proportions and succeeded in building the large dome with a diameter of one hunred and one feet and a height at the center of one hundred and sixty feet. Unfortunately, the dome imploded during an earthquake and was replaced just before the end of Justinian's rule, in 562. The final dome kept the same diameter with a higher center soaring to one hundered and eighty-two feet.

The Hagia Sophia was built to be the center of the Byzantine world. Justinian brought the interior green marble from Thessaly, black stone from the Bosporus, and yellow stone from Syria. Internal columns were transported from the Temple of Artemis at Ephesus.

Justinian II added decorative and figurative mosaics to the walls. The mosaics seen today were created from the late ninth century, after the iconoclast periods. Christ, the saints and church fathers are amply represented, as are Justinian and Empress Theodora. Later monarchs Constantine IX and Empress Zoë flank Christ, surrounded in gold tile. Some mosaics were lost in an earthquake in 1894. These have been replaced in part with paintings.

Interior Suleimaniye Mosque showing calligraphic inscriptions

Massive walls of Hagia Sophia above city walls built by Constantine

Sometime in the ninth or tenth century, Vikings visited Constantinople. Vikings were great travelers. There were Viking mercenary soldiers in the army of the emperor of Byzantium. One Viking visiting the Hagia Sophia was so taken by the largesse and splendor of the place that he recorded his presence by a little graffiti. Etched into the marble is the inscription in rune, the script of Vikings, *Ulf was here.*

When the doge of Venice came to Constantinople in the Fourth Crusade of 1204, relics held and displayed in the Hagia Sophia were taken by crusaders. Decades later, a stone marker was placed in the floor of the repaired Hagia Sophia, as though it was the tomb of Enrico Dandolo, the Venetian doge in command of the sacking. It was a popular place to stand, in a dark corner, for personal relief. Locals discretely and humorously paid their respects to the doge. Archaeological investigation in the nineteenth century revealed that the tomb was more symbolic than actual.

Tribute to Dandolo, Doge of Venice, in a dark corner of Hagia Sophia

When the church became a mosque, a minaret was added and then replaced with a taller tower and two additional minarets. Spectacular candles from the conquest of Hungary were brought in the sixteenth century, as were alabaster urns from Pergamum in western Turkey. Mausoleums of sultans Murad III and Mehmet III were built into the complex at that time. Just outside the entrance, an opulent fountain was endowed by Sultan Mahmud in 1740.

Over the eighteenth and nineteenth centuries, the church-turned-mosque received maintenance, and the interior was cleaned and polished. Old candle chandeliers were replaced with oil pendant lamps. Medallions of sayings of the Prophet Mohamed were hung from the walls. After a substantial restoration in 1849, Justinian would have been pleased to see his building, even though it was not a church.

Pigeon Mosque Dome and surrounding Kulliye

Builders of mosques in Istanbul were so impressed by the Hagia Sofia that its basic structural elements were models for fifteenth century and later constructions. Style changes in the shape of arches, repeated domes, and complex campuses were added in mosques. The idea of height and mass to impress residents and visitors with the glory of God became constant features.

In Islam, part of the prayer ritual includes washing hands and feet before entering the mosque for prayer. Fountains built in Istanbul were often ornate, with a gilded overhanging roof and multiple spigots. The fountain area and entrance to the mosque were often enclosed within a long, low walled courtyard, the sahn. Walls of the courtyard of stone were often lined with shady arcades, held up by columns. In some instances, even in the crowded city of Istanbul, the courtyard was a turf-planted garden. The courtyard furnishes a place of respite from the noisy city.

Each mosque has one or more minarets, to call the faithful to prayer five times each day. The major mosque of Istanbul, Sultan Ahmed Mosque, has six minarets. So as not to disregard preeminence of the Great Mosque of Mecca, which also had six minarets, the sultan of Istanbul commissioned a seventh minaret for Mecca. Smaller mosques in Istanbul have two minarets.

Mosques have one or more domes, known as qubba. A dome replicates the vault to heaven of the Prophet. Outside of Istanbul, mosque builders were creative in the placement of the dome. It could be over the entrance, or over a vestibule. In churches repurposed to mosques, the dome over the altar was left in place. The Great Mosque of Jerusalem has a large dome over the rock where the Prophet ascended to heaven on his midnight ride to receive the Qur'an. The dome was originally fully gilded. In mosques of Iraq and Africa, the dome takes a conical shape.

Plaza of the Pigeon Mosque, Mosque of Beyazid II

Sahn of Suleimaniye Mosque Istanbul

In Istanbul, mosques have a riot of domes. Small domes may line the sahn or side rooms of a masjid. Domes were incorporated into vaults of the structure, as extensions of spanning space and rising ceilings. Looking at the Süleimaniye Mosque, or the Mihrimah Sultan Mosque in Istanbul, from the sahn, the courtyard, the ascending rows of domes, culminating with a single large dome, with the crescent at the top, there is a unique statement of place. Domes are iconic features of Ottoman mosque architecture in Istanbul.

Inside the mosque, the focal point is the mihrab, the singular niche in the sidewall, which denotes the direction of Mecca. The mihrab is usually tiled and ornate. Next to the niche is often a wooden pulpit, raised by a ramp or stair, or a balcony. The pulpit is often surrounded by sayings from the Qur'an, painted in elegant calligraphy.

Of the five daily prayers, the first prayer comes at sunrise and the last at dusk, so it is often dark in the mosque. Before electricity, mosques were lit with oil lamps, suspended from ropes or mounted on large metal wheels, to create chandeliers. Today lamps are still hung in the traditional, historical style, although lamps are electric.

A final historical feature of the mosque masjid is the carpeting. In early times, and outdoor settings, the faithful brought small prayer rugs on which to prostrate themselves. Today, mosques often have carpets. Out of respect, shoes are left outside, feet are washed, and the interior rugs are preserved as clean for prayer.

Interiors of mosques may have elaborate decorative features, all iconoclastic in design. Well-funded mosques are opulent with decorative tile, gilded calligraphy, a profusion of lamps and highly crafted rugs. Sponsors of mosques show piety and give thanks by donations to the community mosque.

In Istanbul, masjids are within külliye, a complex of community service buildings. These may include a hospital, school, kitchen to serve meals to the poor, tombs of great leaders, political and religious, or meet other needs of the faithful. The entire campus may be quite large, extending the entrance to the masjid and lined with minarets.

Six Minarets of Blue Mosque Istanbul

Detail of Mother's Mosque Istanbul

Architects of the Mosques of Istanbul

The first great mosque architect of Istanbul was Mimar Sinan, who lived from 1490 to 1588. He was a Janissary, one of the elite military forces of the sultan. Trained as an engineer, Sinan built siege equipment, aqueducts and bridges over which to transport heavy artillery, which included cannons. At the age of fifty, he became an architect.

Sinan studied the Hagia Sophia, then built his mosques with a larger internal area, filled with light. His buildings are stout and evoke images of power, like his military works. Inside the mosques are creations of delicate artistry to transmit the eloquence of prayer.

Şehzade Mosque was Sinan's first major project, which so impressed his sponsor, Sultan Süleiman the Magnificent, that Sinan quickly had larger commissions. He became chief architect for the Ottoman Empire. His designs set the style replicated in mosques for the next century.

In designing Şehzade Mosque, Sinan experimented with dome placement and support. His initial effort has one main dome and four half-domes. The architect learned that he needed to layer the domes for structural support. Once the physics of dome placement was resolved, there was no end to the number of domes he could work into a design. Domes sitting on rings of windows brought light into the masjid. The white interior, with red marble accents of Şehzade Mosque, created a space full of bright light.

To support high, heavy walls of the main masjid, Sinan used exterior buttresses, much like European cathedrals. He hid the buttresses with columned porticos running down the sides of the main building. External areas under porticos became side rooms in Sinan's later designs.

Woman's section in a Mosque

Layered Domes of the Blue Mosque

The entry courtyard, with the central fountain, the sahn, was lined with an arcade, topped with alternating pink and white marble domes. The whole complex encompassed the tomb of the prince, two schools, and a public kitchen. There was also an adjacent inn for travelers coming to the mosque to give prayer in the name of the prince. Each design element became a standard feature in later mosques, with larger and more numerous domes and extensive complex rooms.

Sinan worked as chief architect of sultans for forty years, living to one hundred years old. He built several mosques, as well as public works and infrastructure of Istanbul. His students became the generation of architects, whose work proliferated over the empire during its glory years.

Garden Entrance to Sahn of Suleimaniye Mosque Istanbul

Sinan Ottoman style was replicated to the extent there were sponsors able to build such glorious mosques. Smaller mosques, without schools, still incorporated the arched arcade of columns in the entry courtyard, at the center of which is a fountain. Arches and vaults, holding massive weight, appear like arabesques of light and color. It is no wonder that the great sultan had a fondness for the great architect, who gave the Ottoman Empire its now classic style.

Ottoman Era Mosques of Istanbul

There are many more mosques in Istanbul than those mentioned here. A visitor could make several trips to Istanbul, enjoy several shore excursions to several mosques, and still be overwhelmed by the experience. The mosques highlighted here are notable for their architecture and art, or the sultan who built them, or both.

FATIH MOSQUE: The first mosque built by Sultan Mehmet II was the Fatih Mosque, also known as the Mosque of the Conqueror. It was built in 1471, on the site of Constantine's Church of the Holy Apostles, after the Christians deemed the original building uninhabitable. Mehmet's tomb was placed in this mosque. The mosque design is based on symmetry and order rather than function. In 1677, the building was heavily damaged in an earthquake. It was repaired in 1776, toward the end of the empire, when there were fewer funds for opulent decoration. The structural symmetry is preserved, lacking much of the décor.

MOSQUE OF BEYAZID II: Mehmet's son built three public complexes that included mosques, one of which is in Istanbul. The Hagia Sophia inspired the mosque built in 1506, although this mosque is half the size. The courtyard attracts pigeons, thus the popular name of Pigeon Mosque. The masjid is in the center of a complex that included schools, hospitals, asylums and meeting places.

SULTAN SELIM MOSQUE: From 1520 to 1522, a mosque was built to honor Selim I, the father of Sultan Suleiman the Great, who died in 1521. The mosque is not a notable architectural achievement. It is known for the tiles crafted in a decorative second glaze technique.

ŞEHZADE MOSQUE: Construction of the Şehzade Mosque in 1548, began a period of imperial mosques built by chief Ottoman architect, Sinan, the father of Ottoman architecture. Often called the Prince Mosque, it was commissioned by Suleiman the Magnificent to honor his son, who died while returning from battle in Hungary. The mosque has two minarets and the symmetrical design characteristic of Sinan architecture. The one main dome has four half-domes. The mosque is notable for its inner beauty in red and white.

SÜLEIMANIYE: Sinan built his next mosque to be worthy of the sultan for whom it was dedicated, Suleiman the Magnificent. It took from 1550 to 1557, to complete the complex. The sultan and his architect carefully considered every detail.

NUMBERS WERE IMPORTANT TO SÜLEIMAN. He was the fourth sultan in the dynasty since the conquest of Constantinople, so his mosque has four minarets. Süleiman was the tenth sultan in the dynasty, so there are ten balconies. Ten columns were removed from the Hippodrome on the central plaza of Istanbul and incorporated into his mosque. One hundred and thirty-eight stained glass windows provided greater light to shine on daily prayers than in the Hagia Sophia.

BLUE MOSQUE: Between 1609 and 1617, a pupil of Sinan built the Blue Mosque, actually named the Mosque of Sultan Ahmet. The blue moniker comes from the floor to ceiling use of blue and white tile. The dome of the large mosque amid half-domed roofs that surround it, make the Blue Mosque as much of a landmark for tourists today as it was for seventeenth and eighteenth century pilgrims to the Holy Land arriving at Istanbul.

Five ornate bronze gates lead to the courtyard surrounding the Blue Mosque on three sides. Twenty-six granite columns are supporting thirty cupolas lining the way into the mosque. Four massive, fluted columns support the main dome.

YENI VALIDE, NEW MOSQUE: The New Mosque was the last of the great mosques of the Ottoman Empire to be built in Istanbul. Begun in 1598, it was not completed until 1663. The sultan who dedicated the mosque to his mother died before its completion. It was completed seven sultans later with funds from the later sultan's mother. Perhaps the donation came hoping that beautiful mosques would continue to be built for mothers.

The mosque is tucked away in buildings that have encroached over the centuries. The entry courtyard and masjid are not large. What the New Mosque lacks in size it more than compensates for in the beauty of its tiles and lamps.

The exterior courtyard and the interior are lavishly tiled in floral and geometric motifs. Inside there are sculpted grills that front the upper balconies. If a walking tour of mosques is part of a port excursion, even a tired traveler will be delighted to be treated to this treasure of Turkish art.

Visiting the Mosques Today

Most visitors to Istanbul stop in the Blue Mosque and the Hagia Sofia. A day in Istanbul can be overwhelming. Mosques are only part of the exquisite cultural features of the city.

Beyond the spice bazaar and palace, the features near the Golden Horn, there are gems of mosques throughout the city, many of which are seldom visited by cruise guests. On a repeat visit to Istanbul, having visited the main sights, wander the streets, away from the crowds, to visit older mosques, the efforts of Sinan. In quiet, garden courtyards take the opportunity to reflect on the weight of domes and walls, built over five hundred years ago, without computers and heavy machinery. In few structures of the world are heavy walls teamed with delicate inlay and tiles to give a light and artistic effect, with so little interior furnishings.

For some, a visit to a mosque in Istanbul is a religious experience. For others, the visit is an experience in history and art. Each mosque has replicated elements, yet each has its personality. In the details of design, lie symmetry and calm. Istanbul has always been a busy place. Enjoy the impact realized by the sultans. They all had power. They appreciated beauty.

Sultans' Mothers Mosque showing mihrab, niche indicating direction of Mecca

Orphic Mysticism, Ovid's Metamorphoses and Modern Turkey

In the cosmos of ancient Greece, Orpheus descended into the underworld. In Thrace, the northern section of ancient Greece, from which people came to the Black Sea, they traveled to unknown worlds, a dark and mysterious land, populated by hostile bands. They spoke of Orpheus as a god. Orphic poetry became a religious mantra, to which people clung in their darkness.

Roman poet Ovid was banished from Rome to ancient Tomis, now known as Constanta, in 8 CE. He considered his sentence worse than joining Orpheus in the underworld. His just-completed text, *Metamorphoses*, is a winding path through the cosmos of ancient Rome. Images drawn in the book are so vivid that fourteen hundred years later, they became the inspiration for themes of artists in what is today known as Renaissance art. Before Biblical allegory was given vision, the imagery on canvas largely came from Ovid. Before the Bible, *Metamorphoses* was a best seller.

Ports of the Black Sea were at the center of commerce in the ancient world. In the religious world of Christendom and Islam, ports of the Black Sea were at the center of competition for control of the routes of commerce. Ancient ways of Greeks, from which they derived stability and put order in their lives, were in contrast to the growing social order of Islam. Each group defined community relationships with certain expectations. For each, uncertainty was minimized.

While ports of the Black Sea remained entrenched in ancient ways, Europe experienced a Renaissance. A new world was discovered across the Atlantic Ocean, giving greater dimension to the globe. European economies became industrialized and specialized. The Black Sea was largely immune to changes occurring in Europe.

◄ *Home of Attaturk now a museum*

To put in perspective the realm of the Black Sea, at the turn of the twentieth century, is to more fully appreciate a leader who transitioned the developing nation of Turkey into a modern state. That man is Kemal Atatürk. His struggle to separate church or mosque and state, as a necessary predicate to a well-functioning political nation, was undertaken with great effort. A century later, reviewing from whence Turkey came may illuminate the critical nature of decisions it makes today.

This itinerary around ports of the Black Sea floats full circle to the channel connecting it to the Mediterranean and other destinations that await. Istanbul is a gateway to Europe. Before departing the Black Sea, with memories of the historical legacy of its unique characters, pause to consider their thoughts. This is a short romp through Orphic Mysticism, Ovid's Metamorphoses, and Atatürk's vision of Modern Turkey.

Altar to gods in Greek Chersonesos, outside Sevastopol

Ancient Greek Orphic Mystery

Orpheus descended into the dark underworld to emerge with spring. Greeks came to the Black Sea 2,800 years ago to plant grain to send home to a hungry Athens. Seeds went into the ground, and farmers went before their altars in Chersonesos, Tomis and elsewhere to ask the gods for a good crop.

People initiated into Orphic mystic practice understood the physical body was possessed of a soul. At death, the body burned or decayed, and the soul traveled to be reborn in a new host. Sins of past lives traveled with the soul. Ancient Greeks sought in life to be purged of their original sin.

Persephone, a goddess of the underworld, traveled among souls, to harass them for their deeds in life for which they were cursed. The knowledge that Persephone awaited all mortals in death was cause to lead a virtuous life.

In 500 BCE, a Greek living in south-central Sicily, Empedocles, wrote volumes about the basic elements of life: water, soil, fire and wind. Fully imbued with Orphic thinking, he paraded up to Mt. Vesuvius with his followers trailing to witness his death and rebirth. When Empedocles jumped, velvet robes and all, into the volcano, only one copper sandal was blown skyward by the fiery blast of air. There was no opportunity for a second opinion. The sandal evidenced a mortal in the volcano, not a god. Empedocles proved he was not to be reborn.[105]

Orphic poems written in parchment and encased in gold amulets on chains, to be worn around the neck for luck, have been found in archaeological sites on the north coast of the Black Sea. Poems remind the wearer that in life, they must not forget death. They must strive to remember and contemplate truthfulness when in death, to emerge knowing in the next life.

Orphic revelers loved their wine. Intoxication brought a clear-headed ability to think deeply. Lacking inhibitions when imbibing was thought of as being closer to the gods. Farmers planted fields of wheat; then, they planted vineyards. When Romans arrived, they fostered a legacy of vineyards. Ceremonies of purification in life included drinking wine.

---

[105] For the story of Empedocles, see Cruise through History, Itinerary II Rome to Venice at the port of Agrigento.

In its most enthusiastic form, Orphic practice developed a ritual, where only the initiated could learn the means to emerge from the life-to-death-to-life cycle in an improved state. Pause when visiting alters in homes of archaeological sites, such as in Chersonesos, to imagine the wine consumed when giving deference to Persephone. Enjoy virtuous feelings that come forth with such clarity when drinking wine. It is easy to understand how Romans appreciated Orphic thinking when they arrived to control Greek wine trade and imbibed with enthusiasm in life.

Ovid's Metamorphoses

Of the top two poets of ancient Rome, one was deified and the other was exiled. Virgil wrote epic poems of the grandeur of Rome until his death in 19 BCE. At the time of Virgil's death, Ovid was twenty-four and writing love poems to numerous women. Inspired by Virgil's epic odes to Augustus Caesar, Ovid switched to collecting the body of Roman history as material for his epic poetry.

Virgil was a court favorite of Augustus Caesar. The poet wrote odes of praise to his sponsor, even though Caesar confiscated lands of Virgil's family to redistribute to his military as bonuses for meritorious service. Virgil did not mind losing the family farm. He was never a robust fellow and had no interest in farming. He wrote of bucolic *Arcadia* and the epic poem *Aeneid*, to justify the rise to power of the nephew of Julius Caesar, his patron, who was more cunning than able as an administrator of an empire.

Virgil died in Brindisi, an Adriatic Sea port utilized by travelers from Greece across the extension of the Via Appia, then an obscure outpost of the Roman military. He is most remembered in Naples, for his prediction that the city would remain protected by the gods as long as the gilded egg in a cage remained unmolested deep beneath the castle in the old port. In 79 CE, Mount Vesuvius spew deadly ash on Pompeii, across the bay. Naples was spared. The Egg Castle is an iconic landmark in Naples today.[106] By the tenth century,

---

[106] See the story of Virgil and the Egg Castle in Cruise through History© Itinerary II Rome to Venice, Port of Naples.

Virgil was deified by some Christians, who considered him the first Christian for his prediction in poetry that a child would be born to bring peace to the world. Legends spread of the miraculous birth of Virgil as a full-grown adult.

When Ovid switched his form to historic epic poetry, he was a happily married man, who only wrote intimate love poems to his wife. As a man of comfortable means, who had achieved considerable fame in the empire, he wished only to solidify his position in the court of Augustus Caesar by writing the history of the Roman Empire to the time of Augustus, eclipsing Virgil.

The magnum opus of Ovid was the *Metamorphoses*, written in Latin, and completed in the fateful year for Ovid of 8 CE. Much longer than Virgil's *Aeneid*, *Metamorphoses* begins fifteen books with the creation of the universe, as it was then known, and runs through time to the ascent of Caesar to a Roman deity. Ovid included his exhaustive description of two hundred and fifty Roman myths and legends. The star at the top of the cosmos was his sponsor, Augustus Caesar.

Ovid was not the only Roman collecting metamorphosis myths in epic poetry. Romans built upon Greek epic poems describing development of the cosmos through the interplay of the pantheon of Greek gods. Length and breadth of *Metamorphoses* distinguish Ovid's effort. It was also considered a quality achievement in its application of the meter of Greek-style recited poetry. Not to be outdone by any poet before him, or to leave any area of literature unaddressed, included in *Metamorphoses* are comedy and tragedy, an elegy to great leaders and bucolic descriptions of landscapes, evocative of Virgil. As a result, *Metamorphoses* is more than a book of evolving subject matter. It represents an evolution of form.

Ovid's chronology is unbroken in a stream of events. More recent scholars have sectionalized the lines into four parts or themes. Much of the first two books are seen as inspiration for Dante's *Divine Comedy*, of human interaction with descent into or emergence from the underworld. Books three through six tell of antics of avenging gods. The middle of book six through the end of book eleven return Ovid to themes of love and books twelve through fifteen deify Augustus Caesar.

The objective of metamorphosis literature is to chronicle the growth of a central character. In Ovid's work, there is no single protagonist, who fails and falls, then succeeds to reach a goal. Rather, Ovid rambles through events, tied together, if at all, by love. The crowning glory of Rome, inheritor of the empire, and guardian of the legacy of Roman civilization is the emperor of Rome, Caesar. *Metamorphoses* is the expression of all of Ovid's desires in a single testament.

Unfortunately for Ovid, his proximity to power exposed him to palace intrigue. The fatal act leading to his exile from Rome, has never been identified. The most that can be surmised is that a young member of the royal family, involved in treasonous acts, implicated Ovid as a participant, or at most, an advisor to a participant. Torn from his wife and daughter, exiled from Rome to Tomis, a sparse farm-town on the Black Sea, was torture worse than death. He never returned.

Out of sight in the Black Sea city, so far from Rome, Ovid was not out of his mind. *Metamorphoses* was widely read and enjoyed. Most stunning of Ovid's achievement was his ability to take storylines he heard since childhood and retell them in colorful detail. His descriptions conjured vivid mental pictures of gods and their interaction with mortals and each other.[107]

Roman art in Ovid's time was cast in the mold of classical Greek style. Romans built roads, aqueducts and major civic structures. Art in sculpture, mosaic and fresco was stylized rather than expressive. A full appreciation of Ovid came over a millennium after his death.

In the thirteenth century, far afield from Rome in Florence, a Renaissance in art, literature and architecture was bursting forth. Dante Alighieri, writing in 1300, from Ravenna, where he sought to retreat from Florence, wrote his *Inferno*, a graphic depiction of the levels of purgatory as souls advanced to, or from, the descent into hell. Anyone familiar with the *Inferno* will recognize the imagery created of souls in purgatory. Dante's

---

[107] There are several translations of Ovid, with notes, including: A New Verse Translation by David Raeburn, Penguin Classics, London, 2004; Translation by Henry T. Riley, Digireads.com, 2017, available in print.

vision, expressed in writing and so often in paintings ever since, came from the first two books of Ovid's *Metamorphoses*.

William Shakespeare is almost without parallel in his ability to use language to entertain Elizabethan England. His often-quoted phrases have captivated audiences for four hundred years. It may come as a surprise that the speech of Prospero in the *Tempest* is cribbed from Ovid in a speech by Medea in Book VII of *Metamorphoses*. Medea also boils a potent mixture, similar to Macbeth's *hell–broth, thick and slab*.[108]

Shakespeare is credited with themes of comedy and tragedy, often appropriated by generations of new authors to stories built on his enduring plots. Shakespeare looked to folk legends for his inspiration. His characters metamorphose throughout four acts, through human blunders, misconceptions and intrigue to arrive at a point of personal growth. Shakespeare's comedy and tragedy plots can be found in Ovid's *Metamorphoses*.

Art historians look to Ovid as the source of inspiration that unleashed imagery in painting in Florence in the fifteenth century, known as Renaissance Art. In Ovid, Daphne escaped the adoration of Apollo by turning herself into a laurel tree, a theme repeated in Italian Renaissance art. The most famous painting in the Uffizi in Florence is Botticelli's Venus, the imagery of which is credited to Ovid. Titian painted the goddess Diana in 1556, in a depiction illustrating the description by Ovid. For art historians, Ovid presents a foundation for an entire catalog of Renaissance art.

Making Modern Turkey

The man born in 1881 as Mustafa Kemal Pasha, became known as the icon of modern Turkey, Kemal Atatürk, from 1935 forward.[109] He pried Turkey from provincialism and led it to be a modern, industrialized nation,

---

[108] Riley, at 210.

[109] There are several opinions of his place of birth and family history. Prevailing thought is that Atatürk was born in Thessalonica, as were Cyril and Methodius, to a modest Muslim family. He was recognized while a student for intelligence and diligence.

in part, by insistence on a secular state. He banned the Fez and promoted European fashion. The nation acknowledged his leadership when he was voted its first president. As a Turkish institution, Atatürk's ideals became known as Kemalism.

Atatürk began his leadership career in the military of the Ottoman Empire in its last days as a force in World War I. He led the battle against the Allied forces in one of its most inglorious defeats of the war at Gallipoli in 1915. As he surveyed the battlefield causalities of mostly Australian and New Zealand forces, the intrepid ANZAC brigades, he is recorded as saying with respect, *they are all our children.*

Transitioning from military leader in World War I to fighter for Turkish independence, Atatürk found himself dealing a mortal blow to the last vestiges of the Ottoman Empire while resisting desires of Allied Nations to divide the large landmass of former Ottoman Turkey into pieces controlled by various of the nations of Britain, France, Italy and Greece. He succeeded on both fronts. To do so, in fifteen years, Atatürk moved with battlefield speed to create a Turkish image of an independent nation, more European than Asian, on the edge of a new world.

Independence of Turkey was not won without some lasting scars. Leading European resistance to an independent Turkey of its present size was the French Foreign Legion, commanding Armenian forces. In the three weeks of the Battle of Marash, Turkish nationalist forces defeated the French and Armenian forces, which led to a massacre of somewhere between five and twelve thousand Armenians. Armenia was also in the process of nation formation. Common boundaries were in dispute.

In 1923, the Treaty of Lausanne, brokered by the United Nations, ended the Greek-Turkish War, resolved independence of the Republic of Turkey, and cleared the way for the election of Atatürk as the first president of the new nation. The Treaty also resulted in expulsion of ethnic Greeks from Turkey to Greece and receipt of ethnic Turks from Greece.[110] Turkish became the only authorized language in Turkey. Atatürk means, father of the Turks.

Within a homogenized Turkish nation, there were disputes between Kemalists and old thinkers. The Kemalist government gave equality and the vote to women. Kemalists appeased the old guard of strict Muslim leaders by imprisoning writers and educators, thought too outspoken and European.[111] Although the departing Ottoman government had a well-developed

---

[110] The ethnic Greeks, from the area of the Black Sea were culturally Turkish in language and dress, although they were mostly Eastern Orthodox Christian who wrote in Greek. The arriving ethnic Turks were Greek in dress and language, although most were Muslim. The UN experiment in ethnic cleansing was an effort to stem bloodshed. The result was further deaths in the abrupt transition, with no support for transferees, and ongoing hostility.

[111] See the Port of Sinop in this Itinerary.

administrative structure, the new and democratic government foresaw the task of establishing legitimacy, by jetisonning Ottoman autocracy, which had been closed to public input. In the newly created void of leadership, the old Caliphate of the Ottomans remained a powerful force within the emerging sovereign nation.

Ottoman Administration Building Sinop

In 1924, the Caliphate and sharia courts were abolished in Turkey. Atatürk had a difficult time assuring other Muslim nations that removing religion from the government was not a lessening of the importance of religion. Education in Turkey was also secularized. Women could attend co-ed schools. In 1934, clothing was secularized, and the veil, turban and fez were relegated to history, although the law was silent on women's head covering, allowing a scarf at the woman's discretion. People's names were secularized and the surname law required families to choose a surname, rather than names bequeathed as a pious Muslim.

In 1928, Arabic script was replaced by a new Turkish alphabet. With a low literacy rate in Turkey, introduction of the new alphabet was an initial introduction to literacy for many Turks. The Qur'an was published in Turkey in Turkish, with the first copy purchased by Atatürk. Turkey proved it could be uniquely Turkish, and still Muslim, in a twentieth-century world.

Kemal Atatürk died on November 10, 1938. Fifteen years as leader of the new nation was insufficient to resolve all of the issues of modernization and institutionalize change. Left open were issues of international relations. Atatürk accepted arms from Russia, when battling forces in the formation of the republic, although he renounced communism as incompatible with a religious and independent Turkey.

Atatürk felt resolving issues with Kurds was made more complex by British desires for oil in the region and old-style tribalism within Turkey. He entered into peace pacts with Iran, Iraq and Afghanistan, which resolved borders. With its neighbors, Turkey faced a common enemy in the rise of Mussolini.

World depression in 1929 and World War II were faced by Atatürk, with an eye toward the economic expansion of a rapidly developing workforce within the country. He saw the future in the skies, although he did not live long enough to carry through on the next wave of industrialization. He would have been pleased with the democratization of Turkey in its post-war economic growth.

Sailing Through Mindful Experiences on the Black Sea Today

So little actual evidence exists of the substance of Orphic Mysticism, leaving open territory for present-day spiritual journeys of the mind by New Age cults. The concept of travels of the soul after death and rebirth is a powerful incentive to live a virtuous life, if only to avoid taunts of Persephone. If wine gives clarity to deep thoughts and brings the inner soul closer to the gods, this may explain popularity of the multi-millennia-old practice of wine as a social beverage.

Ovid's telling of Pygmalion, known to musical theatergoers as My Fair Lady, was related on canvas by French painter Jean Raoux in the eighteenth century. Ovid did not invent Roman mythology. It is his written imagery that endures. When translated into English in 1480 by William Caxton, a merchant, writer and the man who introduced the printing press to England, Ovid was reborn to a new millennium of readers, who had no idea how he suffered in Constanta on the Black Sea. Ovid's visions are viewed by all who visit art museums around the world today.

Turkey is today a country dealing with internal and international issues, not unlike those Atatürk faced while president. Whether Turkey advances the Kemalist view of modern Turkey, whether it incorporates ecumenical and ethnic tolerant ideals of a stable nation, which can afford minority opinion, like minority political parties, or retreats to nineteenth-century ideology, remains an open question. For most of the twentieth century, Kemalism was a model of a growing economy and a world political power on the Black Sea coast. Where Turkey heads in the future will be a model for the region.

Mythical or real, hero or pirate, Jason sailed the Black Sea. Tales of Jason inspired Greeks, Romans, European and Asian adventurers to cross the inner sea and create their own stories. Political turbulence has at times kept cruise visitors from entering the Black Sea, just as Greeks were for so long barred from entry, until the Trojan War. This time it is peace along shores of the Black Sea that will enable travel. When the Bospherous is open to full travel along inner shores, ports of the Black Sea will entertain cruise visitors with stunning regional history, easily accessed from cruise ports. Enjoy them all.

INDEX